BROADWAY IN THE SHADOWS

BASED ON THE WORKS OF
O. HENRY AND AL JENNINGS

WRITTEN BY DAVID SALTER

First published in 2006 by Oberon Books Ltd.
521 Caledonian Road, London N7 9RH
Tel: 020 7607 3637 / Fax: 020 7607 3629
e-mail: info@oberonbooks.com
www.oberonbooks.com

A catalogue record for this book is available from the British Library.

ISBN: 1 84002 704 5 / 978-1-84002-704-4

Characters

JENNINGS

PORTER

JIMMY RAIDLER (THE KID)

DICK PRICE

LOUISA

DIAMOND ROBBER

WARDEN COFFIN

SALLY CASTLETON

CHAPLAIN

JACK LOVE

WARDEN DARBY

IRA MARALLAT

MARY

MR EASTON

THE GLUM MAN

MISS FAIRCHILD

FRIO KID

MEXICAN FRANK

MADISON LANE

ROSITA

BERKLEY

YOUNG WOMAN

DOCTOR ARNOLD

BOY

JIMMY VALENTINE

MIKE DOLAN

BEN TURNER

MISS ANNABEL

AGATHA

AGATHA'S MOTHER

MR ADAMS

VAUDEVILLE MANAGER

BOB HART

WINONA CHERRY

STAGEHAND

VINCENTE

SOAPY

COP

DELLA

JIM

MME SOFRONIE

DOCTOR

SUE

JOHNSY

BEHRMAN

WALTER

MISS ROSA

CONVICTS

TRAIN PASSENGERS

GUARDS

CLERKS

SINGERS

PIANIST

MUSIC

ACT ONE
I'm A Good Ol' Rebel

Let Me Fly

Ragtime Cowboy Joe

Cowboy Sounds

Film Noir

Always Leave Them Laughing

Maple Leaf Rag

Battle Hymn Of The Republic

ACT TWO
Strictly Business

Shine on Me

Temptation Rag

The Greatest Creator of Them All

Christmas Carols

Raise Up

The Dyin' Californian

My Wild Irish Rose

Oh Freedom

ACT ONE

I'M A GOOD OL' REBEL

An old man appears. He wears a long dark overcoat and hat.

JENNINGS: You might say a man is defined by the way he treats other people. If he is generous and kind, always giving to the needy, then we say he is good. And if he is vicious and self-serving, preferring to exploit his fellow citizens, why then we say he is wicked. And each and every man is free to choose. But the truth of the matter is we can't always control the events in our lives. Sometimes life's currents prove too strong and we are swept off our feet and out into the wild waters without warning. There we must sink or swim, and no amount of do-gooding will return us to the shore.

For many years, I never had to question such things. Born in a snow heap and reared in a barn, I earned my living grubbing about in alleys and gathering coal off the sandbars of the Ohio River. I lived the life of a stray dog. Nobody told me what to do and nobody troubled about me. I was free.

Then came a powerful surge of water in the shape of Jack Love. My brother Ed had been pursuing a legal career in Charleston and had successfully prosecuted Love over an embezzlement charge. That night, whilst Ed and I were playing pitch at a side table in a popular saloon, Love and an accomplice, Temple Houston, snuck in through the back door. Houston confronted my brother, while Love crept up behind us unseen. He jammed his forty-five against my brother's skull and fired.

When my brother was shot, all that was good and human in me rushed into my throat, cried itself out and died. I sat there with my brother's head in my lap and his blood soaking into my clothes swearing vengeance.

JENNINGS takes off his hat and coat. Underneath, he wears the outfit of a convict.

No amount of forgiveness or patience or charity was going to return me to the shore. Within days I had shot Temple Houston and been sentenced to life imprisonment in the cruellest institution known to man: the Ohio State Penitentiary. My one regret: I would spend the rest of my incarceration knowing Jack Love walked free.

A company of chained CONVICTS sing 'Oh I'm a Good Ol' Rebel' as they return to the penitentiary. They are counted off and JENNINGS is added to the end of the line.

COMPANY: (*Sing.*) Oh, I'm a good ol' rebel,
    Now that's just what I am;
    For this fair land of freedom
    I do not give a damn.
    I'm glad I fought against it –
    I only wish we'd won.
    And I don't want no pardon
    For anything I've done.

    I can't take up my musket
    And fight 'em now no mo',
    But I ain't a-gonna love 'em,
    Now that is certin sho';
    I don't want no pardon
    For what I was and am;
    And I won't be reconstructed,
    I do not give a damn.

SCENE TWO
THE FIRST DAY

JENNINGS in his prison cell.

JENNINGS: My first day inside and I was assigned to the bolt works. This is the hardest labor in the prison. Outside contractors will pay the State about thirty cents a day for the hire of the men. If a given task is not finished on time, the convict is sent to the hole for 'punishment'.

A hose with a nozzle one quarter of an inch in diameter and sixty pounds pressure behind it sends a stream of terrific force at the prisoner. His head is held strapped, and the stream as hard as steel is turned full in the man's face. The pressure compels him to open his mouth and the battering deluge tears down his throat and rips his stomach in two. No man can stand the water twice and live.

'Li'l Jim', a negro, passed my bench that first morning. 'Mr Al, they done give Li'l Jim the water ag'in,' he said, walked a step, and flopped to the ground, a red geyser spouting from his mouth. Before Li'l Jim reached the hospital, he was dead.

STORY
HEARTS AND HANDS

From nowhere, four CONVICTS suddenly appear. They magically pull out boaters. A warm light falls. They form a traditional barbershop quartet. JENNINGS watches them from his cell.

CONVICT BARBERSHOP: Let me Fly
  Oh Let me Fly
  To Mount Zion
  Hallelujah
  Well I never saw the lights since I was born
  Just get ready to fly away
  Everybody keeps a-talkin' about Judgement morn
  Just get ready to fly away

Better get your wings and try them on
Just get ready to fly away
If you wanna be there when they blow the horn
Just get ready to fly away

A train carriage.

MR EASTON: At Denver there was an influx of passengers into the coaches on the eastbound B & M express.

THE GLUM MAN: In one coach there sat a very pretty young woman dressed in elegant taste and surrounded by all the luxurious comforts of an experienced traveler.

MISS FAIRCHILD: Among the newcomers were two young men, one of handsome presence with a bold, frank countenance and manner; the other a ruffled, glum-faced person, heavily built and roughly dressed.

The two were handcuffed together.

THE GLUM MAN: As they passed down the aisle of the coach the only vacant seat offered was a reversed one facing the attractive young woman.

The young woman's glance fell upon them with a distant, swift disinterest; then with a lovely smile brightening her countenance and a tender pink tingeing her rounded cheeks, she held out a little gray-gloved hand.

MISS FAIRCHILD: Well, Mr Easton, if you will make me speak first, I suppose I must. Don't you ever recognize old friends when you meet them in the West?

THE GLUM MAN: The younger man seemed to struggle with a slight embarrassment which he threw off instantly, and then clasped her fingers with his left hand.

MR EASTON: It's Miss Fairchild, isn't it. I'll ask you to excuse the other hand. It's otherwise engaged just at present.

He raises his right hand.

THE GLUM MAN: Mr Easton, with a little laugh, as if amused, was about to speak again

MR EASTON: when the other forestalled him.

THE GLUM MAN: You'll excuse me for speaking, miss, but I see you're acquainted with the marshal here. If you'll ask him to speak a word for me when we get to the pen he'll do it, and it'll make things easier for me there. He's taking me to Leavenworth prison. It's seven years for counterfeiting.

MISS FAIRCHILD: Oh! So that is what you are doing out here? A marshal!

MR EASTON: My dear Miss Fairchild. I had to do something. Money has a way of taking wings unto itself, and you know it takes money to keep step with our crowd in Washington. I saw this opening in the West, and – well, a marshalship isn't quite as high a position as that of ambassador, but…

MISS FAIRCHILD: The ambassador doesn't call anymore.

And so now you are one of these dashing western heroes, and you ride and shoot and go into all kinds of dangers. That's different from the Washington life. You have been missed from the old crowd.

The girl's eyes, fascinated, went back, widening a little, to rest upon the glittering handcuffs.

THE GLUM MAN: Don't you worry about them, miss. All marshals handcuff themselves to their prisoners to keep them from getting away. Mr Easton knows his business.

MISS FAIRCHILD: Will we see you again soon in Washington?

MR EASTON: Not soon, I think. My butterfly days are over, I fear.

MISS FAIRCHILD: I love the West.

She looks out the window.

Mamma and I spent the summer in Denver. She went home a week ago because father was slightly ill. I could live and be happy in the West. I think the air here agrees with me. Money isn't everything. But people always misunderstand things and remain stupid –

THE GLUM MAN: Say, Mr Marshal. This isn't quite fair. I'm needing a drink, and haven't had a smoke all day. Haven't you talked long enough? Take me in the smoker now, won't you? I'm half dead for a pipe.

The bound travellers rise to their feet, EASTON with the same slow smile on his face.

MR EASTON: I can't deny a petition for tobacco. It's the one friend of the unfortunate. Goodbye, Miss Fairchild. Duty calls, you know.

He holds out his hand for a farewell.

MISS FAIRCHILD: It's too bad you are not going east. But you must go on to Leavenworth, I suppose?

MR EASTON: Yes. I must go on to Leavenworth.

The two men sidle down the aisle into the smoker.

Two PASSENGERS in a seat nearby have heard the conversation.

PASSENGER 1: That marshal's a good sort of chap. Some of these western fellows are all right.

PASSENGER 2: Pretty young to hold an office like that, isn't he?

PASSENGER 1: Young! Why – didn't you catch on? The young man is the one going to jail. Did you ever know an officer to handcuff a prisoner to his *right* hand?

PASSENGER 2: Oh!

The PASSENGERS disappear, the lighting fades. We are back in the Ohio Penitentiary once again. JENNINGS is still in his cell.

JENNINGS: No man forgets his first night without freedom. Locked in a walled space four feet by eight, two men sleeping and breathing together soon turn that closet into hell. When the lights go out, you feel yourself forgotten by all the world.

I longed for some kind of escape. There were rumours going about the pen of secret meetings, of a kind of club in which a few men would get together to tell old stories of their bandit days. You see, men in prison hunger for conversation. They'll tell their stories to anyone who will listen.

A small kitchen was concealed behind a false wall in the construction office and the food stolen or bargained from the chief cook in the prison canteen. One Sunday each month three bank robbers, one forger and one safe cracker would meet up in secret to dine like kings.

SCENE THREE
THE RECLUSE CLUB

A small kitchen in which a group of CONVICTS are preparing a meal. It is Christmas. They are hardened men of the prison, one in a chef's hat stirring a soup, another with an apron sifting sugar. A table is being laid for four, furnished with wild flowers.

DIAMOND ROBBER: Let's speed things up here, Jimmy.

JIMMY RAIDLER: I'm going as f-fast as I can.

DICK PRICE: Where's Bill? We need those tomatoes.

LOUISA: Somebody taste this.

LOUISA offers a spoon and DICK PRICE volunteers to taste it.

DICK PRICE: (*Smacking his tongue to LOUISA.*) A little more celery salt.

LOUISA: Now here, I measured it three times.

DIAMOND ROBBER: Pipe down, Louisa. I'm sure it's fine. If Dick passes out, we'll know not to touch it.

They laugh.

LOUISA: (*Muttering.*) Ain't none of you know good food if it crept up and stabbed you in the back.

JIMMY RAIDLER: C'mon Louisa, he didn't m-mean nothing. We all know you're the best cook in the State of Ohio.

DICK PRICE: Where are those tomatoes?

PORTER enters.

PORTER: Gentlemen, I bring you good tidings.

JIMMY RAIDLER: Bill!

PORTER: It's no Christmas turkey, I'm afraid, but it should suit our purposes.

PORTER empties his pockets revealing a bottle of wine, French sardines, deviled ham, green peas and all manner of delicacies.

JIMMY RAIDLER: That's d-dandy, Bill.

LOUISA: It'll do. (*To JIMMY.*) Pass me the ham, would you.

DICK PRICE: Bill, did you happen to bring any tomatoes?

PORTER: I'm afraid it must have slipped my mind. But why don't you rearrange the table. It seems to have been laid for five and not for six.

JIMMY RAIDLER / LOUISA: Six?

DIAMOND ROBBER: We having guests?

PORTER: Well, gentlemen, I got to talking to this new recruit this morning. It seems he's all alone in the pen and I thought our good cheer might extend to a dinner invitation.

LOUISA: Damn it, Bill. We don't have enough food as it is.

PORTER: I know that, I know that. But we'd be shirking our responsibilities if we let this man spend Christmas Eve all by himself. And besides, if anyone can make our viands stretch, it's you Louisa.

LOUISA: I might be able to make a gumbo or –

PORTER: Wonderful, that's the spirit.

LOUISA: Now hang on, I said I might be able –

DIAMOND ROBBER: I think it sounds like a great idea.

DICK PRICE: Me too.

JIMMY RAIDLER: C'mon, Louisa I'll g-give you a hand.

PORTER: Marvelous. Now unless there are any objections? Let's get to work.

LOUISA: Ridiculous, cooking for six in this little space.

JIMMY RAIDLER: Say, Bill. You thought any more about my idea?

PORTER: I'm considering it.

JIMMY RAIDLER: C'mon, it'll make the story *go*.

DIAMOND ROBBER: You want him to kill a man off every paragraph? If he follows your advice, there'll be nobody left on earth.

JIMMY RAIDLER: A story ain't no good unless there's a hero in it. My hero's k-killed thirty men by page twelve.

They laugh.

DIAMOND ROBBER: You writing a story, Jimmy?

JIMMY RAIDLER: I'm working on something.

PORTER: Good for you, son.

DIAMOND ROBBER: Yes it is. I'm curious about one thing though. How come you know how to write a story but you can't read one?

They laugh.

JIMMY RAIDLER: I never said I got to that part. I'm still at the i-ideas stage.

PORTER: And you've killed thirty men by page twelve? That's quite an idea. You not leaving your hero much time for other forms of entertainment, Jimmy?

JIMMY RAIDLER: Like wh-what?

PORTER: Like a girl, for instance.

JIMMY RAIDLER: Oh he's got a girl.

DIAMOND ROBBER: Then I hope he's old enough to grow whiskers. I ain't heard of no girl taking an interest in young boys before.

JIMMY RAIDLER: What are you talking about? I got a girl waiting for me when I get out.

DIAMOND ROBBER: Sure you do, Jim.

JENNINGS appears.

JENNINGS: Good evening, gentlemen. Would I be right in believing this is the famed Recluse Club?

PORTER: You most certainly would. Gentlemen, this is Al Jennings, a financier worthy to sit with the select. The Colonel here kills with a deft equanimity equaled only by the finesse of Louisa in seasoning the gravy. Welcome to the Recluse Club, Colonel.

DICK PRICE: Good to meet you, Al. Say, do you like tomatoes?

JENNINGS: Right now, I'll eat anything that isn't covered in maggots.

DIAMOND ROBBER: Well, I'd steer clear of Louisa's cooking then.

PORTER: Louisa, don't you rise to it. (*To JENNINGS.*) Now I think it's time for a little toast. Slither over here Colonel and find yourself a seat.

The CONVICTS gather round the table with odd glasses and beakers full of wine.

My fellow troubadours, as a young man it would please me to go serenading at the windows of all the fair maidens in Austin, Texas. Nothing would give me greater pleasure than to strap a harp on my back and saunter from castle to castle living in the gracious beauty of poetry and music. Now it is a sadness to me that my wandering days are over, and the dungeon we find ourselves in has neither drawbridge nor castle. Nonetheless, let us imagine ourselves a happy band of minstrels reclining on some distant patch of grass, and with the little that we have, let us weave fantastic dreams to lighten the drab heart of the men.

And so I propose to read a little scrap I have prepared.

JIMMY RAIDLER: Is it the story, Bill? Is it finished?

PORTER: It is and I'd appreciate the opinions of my fellow strugglers. May I, gentlemen?

The prisoners look to one another, embarrassed and excited.

(*To JENNINGS.*) With your permission?

JENNINGS: Please.

PORTER sits with the men. A harmonica is played.

STORY
A CHAPARRAL CHRISTMAS GIFT

PORTER: The original cause of the trouble was about twenty
years in growing. It possessed a quantity of jet-black hair, a
pair of extremely frank, deep-brown eyes and a laugh that
rippled across the prairie like the sound of a hidden brook.
The name of it was Rosita McMullen.

There came riding on red roan steeds two wooers. One
was Madison Lane, and the other was the Frio Kid. But at
that time they did not call him the Frio Kid, for he had not
earned the honors of special nomenclature. His name was
simply Johnny McRoy.

Madison Lane won the race and he and Rosita were
married one Christmas day. But while the wedding feast
was at its liveliest there descended upon it McRoy, bitten
by jealousy. 'I'll give you a Christmas present,' he yelled,
shrilly, at the door, with his forty-five in his hand. His first
bullet cut a neat underbit in Madison Lane's right ear. The
barrel of his gun moved an inch. The next shot would have
been the bride's had not one of the sheepmen hurled his
plate of roast venison and frijoles at McRoy, spoiling his
aim. The guests spurned their chairs and jumped for their
weapons. It was considered an improper act to shoot the
bride and groom at a wedding. That night was the birth
night of the Frio Kid. The rejection of his suit by Miss
McMullen turned him to a dangerous man.

CONVICTS: (*To 'Ragtime Cowboy Joe'.*)
Out in Arizona where the bad men are
And the only friend to guide you is an evening star
The roughest, toughest man by far
Is the misbegotten Frio Kid

How they run
When they hear the fella's come
That's why the western folks all hid

From the high fallutin'
Rootin' tootin'
Son of a gun from Arizona
The misbegotten Frio Kid

PORTER: The Frio Kid would turn up in towns and settlements, raise a quarrel, pick off his man then laugh at the officers of the law. He was so cool, so deadly, so rapid that none but faint attempts were ever made to capture him. They say he never had mercy on the object of his anger.

CONVICTS: How they run
When they hear the fellas come
That's why the western folks all hid
From the high fallutin'
Rootin' tootin'
Son of a gun from Arizona
The misbegotten Frio Kid

PORTER: Yet at this and every Christmastide it is well to give each one credit for whatever speck of good he may have possessed. If the Frio Kid ever did a kindly act or felt a throb of generosity in his heart it was once at such a time and season, and this is the way it happened.

One December there rode the Frio Kid and his co-murderer, Mexican Frank.

The FRIO KID appears in Santa costume with MEXICAN FRANK. He plays with a gun.

FRIO KID: I don't know what I've been thinking about, Mex, to have forgot all about a Christmas present I got to give. I'm gonna ride over and kill Madison Lane in his own house, tonight.

MEXICAN FRANK: Ah, shucks, Kid, don't talk foolishness. You know you can't get within a mile of Mad Lane's house tonight.

FRIO KID: He got my girl – Rosita would have had me if he hadn't cut into the game. Yes, sir, on Christmas Eve he got her, and then's when I'll get him.

MEXICAN FRANK: There's other ways of committing suicide. Why don't you go and surrender to the sheriff?

FRIO KID: I'll get him I tell you. I wonder why I happened to overlook it up to now.

The FRIO KID conceals the gun in a pocket.

PORTER: Christmas Eve fell as balmy as April. The five or six rooms of the ranch house were brightly lit and in one room stood a Christmas tree. A dozen or more guests were expected from the nearer ranches.

Elsewhere, MADISON LANE appears.

Madison Lane called aside Berkley and some other cowboys employed on his ranch.

MADISON LANE: Now, boys, keep your eyes open. All of you know the Frio Kid. If you see him, open fire without asking questions. Rosita's been afraid he'd pay us a visit every Christmas since we were married. I've a bad feeling about tonight.

PORTER: But no one saw or heard anything. The evening went along pleasantly and the Christmas tree delighted the youngsters, as did Santa Claus himself, who appeared in magnificent white beard and furs to distribute the toys.

When things calmed down, Madison went into the bedroom in search of his wife.

MADISON LANE: (*Disappearing into bedroom.*) Rosita? You in here?

PORTER: This was the moment the Frio Kid was waiting for. But as he followed Madison in to the bedroom to kill him…

The FRIO KID is stopped by the following conversation.

BERKLEY: Well, Mrs Lane, it looks like the Kid ain't coming after all. Maybe you've gotten over being afraid of him now?

ROSITA: Very nearly but I am still nervous sometimes. I shall never forget that awful time when he came so near to killing us.

BERKLEY: He's one cold-hearted villain, all right.

MADISON LANE: (*In bedroom.*) Hey, Rosita! Get in here.

The FRIO KID, can be seen toying with his gun, his eye on MADISON who cannot be seen. ROSITA's words hold him back.

ROSITA: I'm coming.

He has committed awful crimes but – I don't know. I think there is a spot of good somewhere in everybody, don't you Berkley? He was not always bad – that I know.

The FRIO KID disappears into MADISON's room.

BERKLEY: No, Mrs Lane. I don't believe there's any good in that villain. The citizens all along the border ought to turn out and hunt him down like a wolf. That's my opinion.

BERKLEY leaves. As ROSITA turns to enter her bedroom, she bumps into the disguised FRIO KID returning from the room.

ROSITA: Oh, excuse me.

FRIO KID: I heard what you said through the window, Mrs Lane. I was just going down in my pocket for a Christmas present for your husband. But I changed my mind.

He fingers the gun in his pocket. He lets it go.

I left one for you, instead. You'll find it in the bedroom there.

ROSITA: Oh, thank you. Kind Santa.

The FRIO KID leaves. MADISON appears from the bedroom.

MADISON LANE: Who was that?

ROSITA: Where is my present? Santa said he left something for me in here?

MADISON LANE: Haven't seen anything in the way of a present. Unless he could have meant me?

They smile at one another and kiss. The scene fades. We are back in the kitchen. PORTER has disappeared. The men are now eating.

JIMMY RAIDLER: (*With tears in his eyes.*) Damn, Porter. I never knew what a tear looked like till now.

DICK PRICE: I still don't get it.

JENNINGS: (*Opening the wine.*) The Kid decided not to kill Madison Lane at the last minute. He gave Rosita Lane her husband's life by way of a gift.

DIAMOND ROBBER: Which would never happen.

JIMMY RAIDLER: Sure it would.

DIAMOND ROBBER: Uh-huh. If you ask me, Madison Lane had it coming to him. The kid should have shot him when he had the chance.

JIMMY RAIDLER: What do you think, Al?

JENNINGS: I think it makes a nice story.

DIAMOND ROBBER: He means it's not realistic. He knows what would happen if, say, his brother's killer walked through that door right this second. No kind words would stop you doing the right thing for Jack Love, then. Ain't that true, Al?

The others look at JENNINGS briefly, then continue their work.

JIMMY RAIDLER: Well Al's in here and Love's out there, so it makes no difference what he'd do.

DIAMOND ROBBER: (*Making a gesture with his knife across his throat.*) There's only one way to deal with someone like that.

JENNINGS takes off his apron and leaves them at the kitchen table.

SCENE FOUR
FRIENDSHIP IN THE PENITENTIARY

JENNINGS: Bob was a diamond robber and one of the hardest crooks in the pen. Before his arrival in Ohio, he and a friend happened across a rather fancy diamond necklace, which they appropriated with the express intention of generating a little money. Sadly Bob got fingered for the necklace and sent to Ohio, while his friend and accomplice escaped with the goods. Yet no amount of punishment from the authorities could force from Bob the location of his treasure or the identity of his accomplice.

See Bob was a man of his word. He stacked everything on friendship and expected the same in return. 'Friendship,' he'd growl, 'is important. It's worth dying for'.

The DIAMOND ROBBER leaves the kitchen table.

You might understand better if you knew the queer circumstances that landed Bob in the pen in the first place.

STORY
AFTER TWENTY YEARS

A spotlight on the DIAMOND ROBBER, who plays every part.

DIAMOND ROBBER: The time was barely ten o'clock at night, but chilly gusts of wind with a taste of rain in them had well nigh de-peopled the streets.

The policeman on the beat moved up the avenue impressively.

(*As Policeman.*) Trying doors as he went, twirling his club with many intricate and artful movements, turning now and then to cast his watchful eye adown the pacific thoroughfare, the officer, with his stalwart form and slight swagger, made a fine picture of a guardian of the peace.

When about midway of a certain block the policeman suddenly slowed his walk. In the doorway of a darkened hardware store a man leaned, with an unlighted cigar in his mouth. As the policeman walked up to him the man spoke up quickly.

(*As Bob.*) It's all right, officer. I'm just waiting for a friend. It's an appointment made twenty years ago. Sounds a little funny to you, doesn't it? Well, I'll explain if you'd like to make certain it's all straight. About that long ago there used to be a restaurant where this store stands – 'Big Joe' Brady's restaurant.

(*As Policeman.*) Until five years ago. It was torn down then.

(*As Bob.*) Twenty years ago tonight. I dined here at 'Big Joe' Brady's with Jimmy Wells, my best chum.

The DIAMOND ROBBER lights his cigar.

(*Still Bob.*) He and I were raised here in New York, I was eighteen and Jimmy was twenty. The next morning I was to start for the West to make my fortune. Well, we agreed that night that we would meet here again exactly twenty years from that date and time.

(*As Policeman.*) It sounds pretty interesting. Rather a long time between meets, though, it seems to me. Haven't you heard from your friend since you left?

(*As Bob.*) Well, yes, for a time we corresponded. But after a year or two we lost track of each other. You see, the West is a pretty big proposition. But I know Jimmy will meet me here if he's alive, He'll never forget. I came a thousand miles to stand in this door tonight, and it's worth it if my old partner turns up.'

The DIAMOND ROBBER opens his jacket to reveal a handsome watch set with diamonds.

(*Still Bob.*) Three minutes to ten. It was exactly ten o'clock when we parted here at the restaurant door.

(*As Policeman.*) Did pretty well out west, didn't you?

(*As Bob.*) You bet! I hope Jimmy has done half as well. He was a kind of plodder, though, good fellow as he was. A man gets in a groove in New York. It takes the West to put a razor-edge on him.

The policeman twirled his club and took a step or two.

(*As Policeman.*) I'll be on my way. Hope your friend comes around all right. Going to call time on him sharp?

(*As Bob.*) I should say not! If Jimmy is alive on earth he'll be here by that time. So long, officer.

(*As Policeman.*) Good-night, sir.

There was now a fine, cold drizzle falling, and the wind had risen from its uncertain puffs into a steady blow.

About twenty minutes the man from the West waited. And then a tall man in a long overcoat, with collar turned up to his ears, hurried across from the opposite side of the street. He went directly to the waiting man.

(*As Tall Man.*) Is that you, Bob?

(*As Bob.*) Is that you, Jimmy Wells?

(*As Tall Man.*) Bless my heart! It's Bob, sure as fate. I was certain I'd find you here if you were still in existence. Well,

well, well! – twenty years is a long time. The old gone, Bob. How has the West treated you, old man?'

(*As Bob.*) Bully; it has given me everything I asked it for. You've changed lots, Jimmy. I never thought you were so tall by two or three inches.

(*As Tall Man.*) Oh, I grew a bit after I was twenty.

(*As Bob.*) Doing well in New York, Jimmy?

(*As Tall Man.*) Moderately. I have a position in one of the city departments. Come on, Bob; we'll go around to a place I know of, and have a good long talk about old times.

The two men started up the street, arm in arm. The man from the West was beginning to outline the history of his career. The other, submerged in his overcoat, listened with interest.

At the corner stood a drug store, brilliant with electric lights. When they came into this glare each of them turned simultaneously to gaze upon the other's face.

The man from the West stopped suddenly and released his arm.

(*As Bob.*) You're not Jimmy Wells. Twenty years is a long time, but not long enough to change a man's nose from a Roman to a pug.

(*As Tall Man.*) It sometimes changes a good man into a bad one. You've been under arrest for ten minutes, 'Silky' Bob. Chicago police thinks you may have dropped over our way and wires us she wants to have a chat with you. Now, before we go on to the station here's a note I was asked to hand you. You may read it here at the window. It's from Patrolman Wells.

The DIAMOND ROBBER hands the note to himself.

'Bob: I was at the appointed place on time. When you struck the match to light your cigar I saw it was the face of a diamond robber wanted in Chicago. Somehow I couldn't do it myself, so I went around and got a plain clothes man to do the job. Jimmy.'

The DIAMOND ROBBER retreats slowly off stage as the music fades away.

We return to the kitchen. JENNINGS, LOUISA and DICK PRICE are playing cards.

DICK PRICE: Did Bill hear anything from that magazine? What was it called?

JENNINGS: 'Everybody's'. And no, he's not heard anything yet.

DICK PRICE: I'd sure like to see the warden's face, knowing he had a published writer in the pen.

JENNINGS: Let's not count our chickens just yet.

JIMMY RAIDLER rushes in clutching a newspaper.

JIMMY RAIDLER: Hey fellas, fellas. You hear what happened? Bob kn-knocked off ol' Maggot.

JENNINGS: The newspaper editor? What did he do?

LOUISA: Whatever it was, he deserves it. That potato-eater would crucify his own mother just to gain a crust.

JIMMY RAIDLER: Seems Bob and Maggot got to talkin' and Bob confided in ol' Maggot where the necklace was st-stashed.

JENNINGS: Where did you hear that?

THE KID throws down a newspaper, defiantly.

JIMMY RAIDLER: Front page headlines.

The others laugh.

LOUISA: 'Police Grab Necklace And Accomplice.'

DICK PRICE: I bet Maggot couldn't stop himself.

JENNINGS: (*To THE KID.*) You got all this from the papers?

JIMMY RAIDLER: Uh-huh.

LOUISA: You been learning to read behind our backs, Jimmy?

JIMMY RAIDLER: One of the bulls told me Bob went to see ol' Maggot this afternoon. Sn- Sneaked down the corridor with a bottle of carbolic acid in his hand and fell into line just as ol' Maggot was returning to his cell. There was a f- fight, then a cry and next thing ol' Maggot's lying on the floor, one eye burned out and his face all smoke and blisters. When he comes out of the hospital, h-hell itself won't own him.

DICK PRICE: They'll kill Bob for this.

JIMMY RAIDLER: Warden's g-gonna give him the seventy-five. Anyways, that's what I heard.

JENNINGS addresses us directly once again.

JENNINGS: The 'Seventy-five' was the punishment ordered for the attack and some of us were made to witness it. Bob was strapped across the trough in the basement, his ankles drawn under it, his arms across the top. He was a mass of blood.

A cold light rises on the punishment cell. The DIAMOND ROBBER is strapped down. Above him stands WARDEN COFFIN and two GUARDS, one of whom holds a bloody paddle.

Long after he was unconscious, the merciless flaying went on. Finally, the guard stopped. Bob came to. The warden glowered over him.

WARDEN COFFIN: C'mon son, this ain't doin' you good. Say that you're sorry and we'll stop all this nonsense.

The DIAMOND ROBBER spits.

Give it to him again.

The GUARD beats the DIAMOND ROBBER.

Why are you doin' this to yourself, boy? I can't have inmates lashing out at one another whenever the feeling takes them. You know that.

Now say that you are sorry. Say that you'll obey the rules.

The DIAMOND ROBBER raises his head.

DIAMOND ROBBER: God damn him. I wish I got his other eye.

A burlesque underscores the torture. The WARDEN turns to the audience and sings 'Always Leave Them Laughing When You Say Goodbye':

WARDEN COFFIN: My dad would never preach to me
In fact he'd never teach to me
The different things that I should do
When I'd be here and there
In fact he said go on alone
You have ideas of your own
You never lose if you will use
The others fair and square

WARDEN COFFIN dances with the GUARDS.

That's just as far as he'd advise
Until one day to my surprise
I went to say that I was going
To other lands to live
And as I went to say goodbye
He saw a teardrop in my eye
Said he, 'My lad, well that's too bad
I've some advice to give.'

The GUARDS rip off their uniforms to reveal burlesque outfits underneath. The WARDEN is in his underwear. The GUARDS flank the warden as he sings. The DIAMOND ROBBER has returned to his trough and is beaten to a grizzly death by the third GUARD.

WARDEN COFFIN:
Always leave them laughing when you say goodbye
Never linger long about or else you wear your welcome out
When you meet a fellow with a tear-dimmed eye
You can leave him laughing if you try
When he tells his troubles
Interrupt him with a joke
Tell him one he's never heard
And he'll declare that's it's a bird
When he's giggling good you know
That's the time to turn and go
Always leave them laughing when you say goodbye

Lights out on the torture.

SCENE FIVE
AN ACT OF KINDNESS

JENNINGS is on his own.

JENNINGS: They called me a killer. I never murdered a man in my life. I shot quick and clean in self-defence. I would have felt myself a degraded beast to kill like that.

Bob's death filled me with rage. The pen was picking us off one by one and meanwhile my brother's killer was roaming free. I tried to escape, got caught and was sent into solitary.

Two weeks later, I was waiting outside Warden Coffin's office. He wanted to know who gave me the tools to escape. Well Porter had helped me get 'em and I sure as hell wasn't about to admit that. Dick Price, the old convict from the Recluse Club, tried to help me.

WARDEN COFFIN: (*Voice.*) Jennings get in here.

DICK PRICE and the WARDEN are in the WARDEN's office.

DICK PRICE: Jennings is a new man, boss. Ain't been here long enough to know the ropes. I gave him the saws, wised him up to escape.

JENNINGS appears.

JENNINGS: Yes, boss?

WARDEN COFFIN: It seems we've found out where you got those saws from.

JENNINGS looks carefully at DICK PRICE. PRICE coughs.

JENNINGS: Dick had nothing to do with it, boss.

WARDEN COFFIN: I thought as much. Get him out of here.

A GUARD leads DICK PRICE out, coughing.

(*Calling after him.*) And go see the croaker. Get that cough seen to!

DICK PRICE: Yes, boss.

DICK PRICE exits.

WARDEN COFFIN: (*To JENNINGS.*) Dick's a good boy. Been here a mighty long time but he can be misguided. Come clean on this now and I'll make it easy for you. Who gave you those saws?

JENNINGS: I found 'em, boss.

WARDEN COFFIN: Don't play games with me, Jennings. Where d'you get 'em?

JENNINGS: I can't tell you, boss.

WARDEN COFFIN: You'll do what you're damn well told. Now who was it?

JENNINGS: I won't rat, boss.

WARDEN COFFIN: Don't push me on this, boy. I'm warning you. I will come down on you like a block of cement. Who was it gave you those saws?

JENNINGS says nothing.

(*To the GUARD.*) Here take this fellow down and give him the seventy-five.

The GUARD grabs JENNINGS.

JENNINGS: You take me, you damn coward; you beat me – and if I live through it, I'll come back and cut your damn throat.

The opening bars of the Maple Leaf Rag are played on the piano as JENNINGS is dragged out to be flogged. The lights change.

STORY
BY COURIER

Two benches. A YOUNG WOMAN appears. She taps her way to the bench. As she arrives, the music suddenly stops. She makes no recognition of having danced to her position.

YOUNG WOMAN: It was neither the season nor the hour when the Park had frequenters; and it is likely that the young lady, who was seated on one of the benches had merely obeyed a sudden impulse to sit for a while. A certain melancholy that touched her countenance must have been of recent birth, for it had not yet altered the fine and youthful contours of her cheek, nor subdued the arch though resolute curve of her lips.

Music. DOCTOR ARNOLD enters, tapping. As before, when he stops moving the music stops.

DOCTOR ARNOLD: A tall young man came striding through the park along the path near which she sat.

Music. A BOY carrying a case enters, tapping. As before, when he stops moving the music stops.

BOY: Behind him tagged a boy carrying a suitcase.

Music. They dance together.

DOCTOR ARNOLD: At sight of the young lady, the man's face changed to red and back to pale again. He passed within a few yards of her,

DOCTOR ARNOLD dances to her then puts on a showy display of tap. Music stops, he looks at her hopefully. The WOMAN sighs. DOCTOR ARNOLD looks to the PIANIST, the music starts he tries again. Music stops. The YOUNG WOMAN yawns.

but he saw no evidence that she was aware of his presence or existence. Some fifty yards further on he sat on a bench.

Music, the BOY and DOCTOR ARNOLD dance to the other bench.

The young man took out his handkerchief and wiped his brow. It was a good handkerchief, a good brow, and the young man was good to look at. He said to the boy:

I want you to take a message to that young lady on that bench. Tell her I am on my way to the station, to leave for San Francisco, where I shall join that Alaska moose-hunting expedition. Tell her that, since she has commanded me neither to speak nor to write to her, I take this means of making one last appeal to her sense of justice, for the sake of what has been. Tell her that to condemn and discard one, without giving him a chance to explain, is contrary to her nature as I believe it to be. Go, and tell her that.

The BOY holds out his hat at the MAN. DOCTOR ARNOLD drops a half-dollar into the BOY's hand.

BOY: The boy looked at him for a moment then set off at a run.

Music. The BOY taps over to the other bench. He is out of breath. Music stops.

The BOY touches the brim of his cap.

Lady, dat gent on de oder bench sent yer a song and dance by me. If yer don't know de guy, and he's tryin' to do de Johnny act, say de word, and I'll call a cop in t'ree minutes. If yer does know him, and he's on de square, w'y I'll spiel yer de bunch of hot air he sent yer.

YOUNG WOMAN: The young lady betrayed a faint interest.

A song and dance!, she said, in a deliberate sweet voice that seemed to clothe her words in a diaphanous garment of impalpable irony. A new idea – in the troubadour line, I suppose. I used to know the gentleman who sent you, so I think it will hardly be necessary to call the police. You may execute your song and dance, but do not sing too loudly. It is a little early yet for open-air vaudeville, and we might attract attention.

BOY: Awe, yer know what I mean, lady. 'Tain't a turn, it's wind.

Music, the BOY taps. Music stops.

He told me to tell yer he's got his collars and cuffs in dat grip for a scoot clean out to 'Frisco. Den he's goin' to shoot snow-birds in de Klondike.

Music, the BOY taps. Music stops.

He says yer told him not to send round no more pink notes nor come hangin' over de garden gate, and he takes dis means of puttin' yer wise.

Music, the BOY taps. Music stops.

He says yer refereed him out like a has-been, and never give him no chance to kick at de decision.

Music, the BOY taps. Music stops.

He says yer swiped him, and never said why.

YOUNG WOMAN: The slightly awakened interest in the young
lady's eyes did not abate. Perhaps it was caused by either
the originality or the audacity of the snow-bird hunter,
in thus circumventing her express commands against the
ordinary modes of communication.

Tell the gentleman that I need not repeat to him a
description of my ideals. He knows what they have been
and what they still are. So far as they touch on this case,
absolute loyalty and truth are the ones paramount.

The PIANIST starts to play, the BOY starts to tap away, but the
YOUNG WOMAN calls him back.

Tell him that I have studied my own heart as well as one
can, and I know its weakness as well as I do its needs.
That is why I decline to hear his pleas, whatever they may
be. I did not condemn him through hearsay or doubtful
evidence, and that is why I made no charge. But, since he
persists in hearing what he already well knows, you may
convey the matter.

The PIANIST starts to play, the BOY starts to tap away, but the
YOUNG WOMAN calls him back.

Tell him that I entered the conservatory that evening
from the rear, to cut a rose for my mother. Tell him I saw
him and Miss Ashburton beneath the pink oleander. The
tableau was pretty, but the pose and juxtaposition were too
eloquent and evident to require explanation.

The PIANIST starts to play, the BOY starts to tap away, but the
YOUNG WOMAN calls him back.

I left the conservatory, and, at the same time, the rose and
my ideal.

The PIANIST and the BOY are unsure whether they can go.

You may carry that song and dance to your impresario.

The PIANIST starts to play, but the BOY stops him.

BOY: I'm shy on one word, lady. Jux – jux – put me wise on dat, will yer?

YOUNG WOMAN: Juxtaposition – or you may call it propinquity.

The BOY is none the wiser.

– or, if you like, being rather too near for one maintaining the position of an ideal.

Music. The BOY taps to the other bench.

BOY: De lady says dat she's on to de fact dat gals is dead easy when a feller comes spielin' ghost stories and tryin' to make up, and dat's why she won't listen to no soft-soap. She says she caught yer dead to rights, huggin' a bunch o' calico in de hot-house. She side-stepped in to pull some posies and yer was squeezin' de oder gal to beat de band. She says it looked cute, all right all right, but it made her sick. She says yer better git busy, and make a sneak for de train.

DOCTOR ARNOLD gives a low whistle and his eyes flash with a sudden thought. His hand flies to the inside pocket of his coat, and draws out a letter, handing it to the BOY.

DOCTOR ARNOLD: Give that letter to the lady and ask her to read it.

The PIANIST starts to play, the BOY starts to tap away, but DOCTOR ARNOLD calls him back.

Tell her that it should explain the situation.

The PIANIST starts to play, the BOY starts to tap away, but DOCTOR ARNOLD calls him back.

Tell her that, if she had mingled a little trust with her conception of the ideal, much heartache might have been avoided.

The PIANIST starts to play, the BOY starts to tap away, but DOCTOR ARNOLD calls him back.

Tell her that the loyalty she prizes so much has never wavered.

The PIANIST starts to play, the BOY starts to tap away, but DOCTOR ARNOLD calls him back.

Tell her I am waiting for an answer.

Music. The BOY taps back to the YOUNG WOMAN.

BOY: De gent says he's had de ski-bunk put on him widout no cause. He says he's no bum guy; and, lady, yer read dat letter, and I'll bet yer he's a white sport, all right.

YOUNG WOMAN: The young lady unfolded the letter; somewhat doubtfully, and read it.

'Dear Dr Arnold: I want to thank you for your most kind and opportune aid to my daughter last Friday evening, when she was overcome by an attack of her old heart-trouble in the conservatory at Mrs Waldron's reception Had you not been near to catch her as she fell and to render proper attention, we might have lost her. I would be glad if you would call and undertake the treatment of her case. Gratefully yours, Robert Ashburton.'

BOY: De doc wants an answer. Wot's de word?

YOUNG WOMAN: The lady's eyes suddenly flashed on him, bright, smiling and wet.

Tell that guy on the other bench, she said, with a happy, tremulous laugh, that his girl wants him.

Music. DOCTOR ARNOLD and the YOUNG WOMAN tap out, happily. A spotlight shrinks on their retreating exit.

A GUARD returns a beaten JENNINGS to his prison cell.

JENNINGS' cell. PORTER calls to JIMMY.

PORTER: Jimmy, would you fetch me some warm soapy water and bandages? There should be something in the pharmacy.

PORTER tends to JENNINGS who is moaning.

All right, colonel. Keep still. It looks as if you've fought the whole Yankee nation single-handed. What were you thinking of? The Warden wouldn't have come down on me too hard, you know that.

JIMMY RAIDLER: (*Returning with the bandages.*) There you go, Bill.

PORTER: Thank you. Now help me get him washed.

A tap dancer passes the time as JENNINGS is washed and cleaned up.

SCENE SIX
A LAND OF OPPORTUNITY

JENNINGS reappears, somewhat the worse for wear.

JENNINGS: It is a popular belief that this country offers every man the chance to better himself. Maybe he won't make president or millionaire, but no matter what the conditions of his birth, a man will have at least one opportunity for advancement.

Dick Price was what convicts call a stir-bug. He'd been in and out of prison ever since he was a little fellow of eleven. One day the ravenous little rag-picker stole a ten-cent box and after his third offence, this time for safe-cracking, Dick was sent to hell for the rest of his life. He was robbed of all human comforts. He couldn't have book or paper and he wasn't allowed to write a letter or even receive one. For forty years not one bit of cheer came to him from the outside world. Then one day, Dick's opportunity came calling.

The Press-Post Publishing Company had been robbed and vital papers locked inside an abandoned safe. They had to get them out. It occurred to somebody that there might be a cracksman in the pen. Everyone knew Dick could open any combination on earth in ten to fifteen seconds. I put his name forward.

Early that afternoon, the Warden got a closed carriage and the three of us went to the office of the Press-Post Publishing Company.

The Press-Post Publishing Company. DICK PRICE appears, coughing occasionally.

He files down his nails as JENNINGS describes.

Dick took out a file and began filing his nails crosswise through the middle. They were deep and beautifully shaped. Back and forth he filed until the lower half of the nail was separated from the upper by a thin red mark. Then he filed down to the quick until only the lower half of the nail remained.

DICK PRICE works the safe and in twelve seconds lets out a gasp. The door to the safe swings slowly outwards.

Everyone was struck dumb. It seemed like a miracle. Warden Coffin's face flushed with pride. He put his arm on Dick's shoulder. That was fine lad. God bless you!

A closed carriage.

On the ride back to the pen, Dick looked out of the carriage window, watching the people and houses.

DICK PRICE: Look at that, look at that. That's the first kid I've seen in sixteen years.

JENNINGS: Dick didn't look out again. We said nothing further during the drive back to prison.

DICK PRICE fades from view.

The next morning every newspaper was full of the sensational story, but the warden had given his word. The process would not be revealed. No one would know a convict had helped save the day.

Meantime Dick's cough was getting pretty bad. Little Jimmy Raidler had been working with Porter in the pharmacy. I went to ask him if there was anything he could do.

The pharmacy. JIMMY is organising the medicines.

JIMMY RAIDLER: I don't know, stock is real low at present. I'll speak to Bill, see if he can't make something up.

JENNINGS: Good boy, Jimmy.

JIMMY RAIDLER: Say, did you see Coffin's face when Dick opened the safe? Way I hear it, looked as if all his Christmases had come at once.

JENNINGS: He'll do well out of it, no doubt.

JIMMY RAIDLER: So how did he manage it? Was it easy?

JENNINGS: Now you know I can't tell you that, Jimmy. I gave my word.

JIMMY RAIDLER: I s-suppose if it was quiet, he could just hear the d-dials turn? Or maybe he sandpapered the balls of his fingers? Is that how he did it? You can tell me, Al. I won't tell a soul.

JENNINGS: I bet not. What are you so interested for, anyway? Planning a new career?

JIMMY RAIDLER: Just curious is all. I guess Dick'll have to start over when he gets out.

JENNINGS: I imagine he will.

WARDEN COFFIN enters.

WARDEN COFFIN: Good evening, gentlemen. Jennings, could I have a word?

JENNINGS: Yes, boss.

JIMMY RAIDLER makes to leave.

WARDEN COFFIN: You might as well hear this too, Jimmy. It's regarding Dick Price.

JIMMY RAIDLER: Is it the p-pardon, boss?

WARDEN COFFIN: I'm afraid not. You see the governor has a very strict policy on the granting of pardons. Very strict.

JENNINGS: Oh.

WARDEN COFFIN: I want you to know, I did everything I could.

JIMMY RAIDLER: So how long's it gonna take?

JENNINGS: There is no pardon, Jimmy.

JIMMY RAIDLER: No pardon? But you told him, boss. You promised.

WARDEN COFFIN: I'm sorry but it's out of my hands. Truly.

The WARDEN exits. Sounds of a penitentiary door slamming shut. The lights change. A colorful prison.

STORY
A RETRIEVED REFORMATION

PORTER: (*Voice-over.*) Figuratively speaking, some people are Backs for burdens, some are Hearts for feelings, some are Heads, some are Bosoms and some are Muscles. Jimmy Valentine was all fingers, and not just for counting.

Jimmy had served only ten months of a four-year sentence. When a man with as many friends on the outside as Jimmy Valentine had is received in the stir it is hardly worthwhile to cut his hair.

CLERK: Jimmy Valentine!

JIMMY VALENTINE is handed his pardon from a CLERK in the prison counter.

There's your pardon Jimmy. It's been signed this morning by the governor.

You also get one railroad ticket, one five-dollar bill and a cigar.

Now, Jimmy, brace up and make a man of yourself. You're not a bad fellow at heart. Stop cracking safes, and live straight.

JIMMY VALENTINE: Me? Why, I never cracked a safe in my life.

CLERK: (*Laughing.*) Oh, no? Of course not. Let's see, now. How was it you happened to get sent up on that Springfield job?

JIMMY lights up his cigar.

JIMMY VALENTINE: Me? Why, I never was in Springfield in my life!

JIMMY blows smoke in the CLERK's face. The CLERK blows out the match.

CLERK: Better think over my advice, Jimmy. Valentine, 9762. Pardoned by governor.

PORTER: (*Voice-over.*) Disregarding the song of the birds, the waving green trees, and the smell of the flowers, Jimmy headed straight for the café of one Mike Dolan, pausing only to fire up a cigar a grade better than the one the warden had given him.

JIMMY sits at the bar of MIKE DOLAN. They shake hands. MIKE is alone behind the bar.

MIKE DOLAN: Sorry we couldn't make it sooner, Jimmy, me boy. But we had that protest from Springfield to buck against, and the governor nearly balked. Feeling all right?

JIMMY VALENTINE: Just fine. Got my case?

MIKE reaches down and pulls out an old suitcase, handing it over to JIMMY, who opens it and gazes fondly at a fine set of burglar's tools.

MIKE DOLAN: Got anything on, Jimmy?

JIMMY VALENTINE: Me? I don't understand. I'm representing the New York Amalgamated Short Snap Biscuit Cracker and Frazzled Wheat Company.

JIMMY slaps a company sticker on his case. They laugh. JIMMY leaves.

A projection shows a series of newspaper headlines spinning down in traditional film style. A spate of burglaries in Richmond, Indiana, Logansport, Jefferson City and so on, with no clue as to the author.

PORTER: (*Voice-over.*) A week after the release of Valentine 9762 there was a neat safe burglary in Richmond, Indiana, with no clue as to the author. Two weeks after that a burglar-proof safe in Logansport was opened like a cheese to the tune of fifteen hundred dollars. The losses were now high enough to bring the matter up into Ben Turner's class of work.

A telephone rings. A MAN emerges from the shadows and answers it.

BEN TURNER: (*On phone.*) That's Dandy Jim Valentine's autograph, all right. He's resumed business. Look at that combination knob – jerked out as easy as pulling up a radish in wet weather. Yes, I want Mr Valentine all right. He'll do his bit this time, without any short-time foolishness that's for certain.

Sounds of a railroad. A voice calls out: 'Elmore. Train stops here. Everybody off.' JIMMY VALENTINE appears.

PORTER: (*Voice-over.*) One afternoon Jimmy Valentine and his suitcase climbed out of the mail-hack in Elmore, Arkansas. Jimmy, looking like an athletic young senior just home from college, passed a young lady crossing the street. Jimmy looked into her eyes, forgot what he was, and became another man. A man all fingers and thumbs.

As he turns, JIMMY bumps into a young lady crossing the street. He helps her up.

JIMMY VALENTINE: Excuse me, miss?

She lowers her eyes and colors slightly. The young lady enters a door over which is the sign 'Adams Bank.'

JIMMY collars a BOY loafing on the steps of the bank.

(*Wily.*) Isn't that young lady Miss Polly Simpson?

BOY: Naw. She's Annabel Adams. Her pa owns this bank. What'd you come to Elmore for? Is that a gold watch-chain? I'm going to get a bulldog. Got any dimes?

JIMMY throws the BOY a dime then enters the Planters' Hotel. He rings the bell.

HOTEL CLERK: Good afternoon, sir. May I help?

JIMMY VALENTINE: You got any rooms in this establishment?

HOTEL CLERK: Certainly sir. If you'd like to sign here?

JIMMY signs.

HOTEL CLERK: (*Handing over a key.*) There you go, Mr Spencer. Room twelve.

JIMMY VALENTINE: Thanks. Say, I'm looking to open up a shoe business here in Elmore. You don't happen to know of any openings, do you?

HOTEL CLERK: As it happens we're lacking a decent shoe store, Mr Spencer. The only place to get them currently is the dry-goods store on Elm Street.

JIMMY VALENTINE: Thank you.

HOTEL CLERK: Let me call the boy to take your case, Mr Spencer.

JIMMY VALENTINE: No. No it's all right. The case is rather heavy. I'll take it up myself.

We watch as JIMMY VALENTINE transforms into Ralph Spencer before our eyes.

PORTER: (*Voice-over.*) Mr Ralph Spencer, the phœnix that arose from Jimmy Valentine's ashes, remained in Elmore and prospered. At the end of a year the situation was this: he had won the respect of the community, his shoe-store was flourishing, and he and Annabel were engaged to be married.

One day Jimmy sat down in his room and wrote this letter:

JIMMY VALENTINE: 'Dear Old Pal, I want you to be at Sullivan's place next Wednesday night. I want to make you a present of my kit of tools. Say, Billy, I've quit the old business. I'm making an honest living, and I'm going to marry the finest girl on earth. I wouldn't do another crooked thing for the whole world. Your old friend, Jimmy.'

JIMMY takes the letter and hands it to the CLERK.

Say, could you get this sent out today?

HOTEL CLERK: How can I help you this morning, Mr Spencer?

JIMMY VALENTINE: Say, could you get this sent out today?

HOTEL CLERK: No problem at all. You have a nice day.

JIMMY VALENTINE: You too, son.

JIMMY leaves as a familiar figure approaches.

BEN TURNER: Excuse me, can you tell me that man's name? I think we went to school together.

HOTEL CLERK: That was Ralph D Spencer, sir. One of the finest citizens of Elmore. This time Monday, he'll be married to Miss Annabel Adams.

BEN TURNER: Any relation to the banker?

HOTEL CLERK: His daughter. Who shall I tell him –

BEN TURNER: No. Don't mention it. I want to surprise him.

JIMMY, MISS ANNABEL, AGATHA and her MOTHER are touring the bank.

MR ADAMS: Ladies and Gentlemen, welcome to Elmore Adams Bank. The vault is a small one, but it has a new, patented door.

There are suitable gasps from the crowd.

It fastens with three solid steel bolts thrown simultaneously with a single handle…

More gasps.

…and has a time-lock.

Final gasp.

Here Ralph, I can show you…

JIMMY's case is in the way so ANNABEL picks it up.

MISS ANNABEL: My! Ralph, how heavy your case is? Feels like it was full of gold bricks.

JIMMY VALENTINE: Lot of nickel-plated shoe-horns in there that I'm going to return. Thought I'd save express charges by taking them up myself. I'm getting awfully economical.

They laugh.

PORTER: (*Voice-over.*) 'Mr Adams beamingly explained its workings to Mr Spencer, who showed a courteous but not too intelligent interest. A young girl, Agatha, was delighted by the shinning metal and funny clock and knobs. Meanwhile...'

GENTLEMAN: Have you seen the new vault?

BEN TURNER: No, thank you. I'm just waiting for a friend.

Suddenly there is a commotion. A woman screams.

MOTHER: My daughter... Agatha's locked in the vault.

MR ADAMS: The door can't be opened. The clock hasn't been wound nor the combination set.

AGATHA'S MOTHER screams again, hysterically.

MR ADAMS: Hush! All be quiet for a moment. Agatha! Listen to me.

During the following silence they can just hear the faint sound of the child wildly shrieking in the dark vault in a panic of terror.

MOTHER: My precious darling! She will die of fright! Open the door! Oh, break it open! Can't you men do something?

MR ADAMS: There isn't a man nearer than Little Rock who can open that door. My God! Spencer, what shall we do? That child – she can't stand it long in there. There isn't enough air, and, besides, she'll go into convulsions from fright.

AGATHA'S MOTHER beats the door of the vault with her hands. Somebody wildly suggests dynamite. ANNABEL turns to JIMMY, her large eyes full of anguish, but not yet despairing.

MISS ANNABEL: Can't you do something, Ralph – try, won't you?

JIMMY looks at her with a queer, soft smile on his lips and in his keen eyes.

JIMMY VALENTINE: Annabel, give me that rose you are wearing, will you?

ANNABEL unpins the bud from her dress, and places it in his hand. JIMMY stuffs it into his vest-pocket, throws off his coat and pulls up his shirt-sleeves. Ralph D Spencer passes away and JIMMY VALENTINE takes his place.

Get away from the door, all of you.

JIMMY opens his suitcase and lays out the shining, queer implements swiftly and orderly, whistling softly to himself. The others watch him as if under a spell.

PORTER: (*Voice-over.*) In ten minutes – breaking his own burglarious record – he threw back the bolts and opened the door. Agatha, almost collapsed, but safe, is gathered into her mother's arms.

JIMMY VALENTINE makes eye contact with BEN TURNER. He puts on his coat, and walks outside toward the front door. As he goes, a far-away voice calls 'Ralph!' but he does not hesitate.

At the door BEN TURNER bars his way.

JIMMY VALENTINE: (*Smiling strangely.*) Hello, Ben! Got around at last, have you? Well, let's go. I don't know that it makes much difference, now.

BEN TURNER: Guess you're mistaken, Mr Spencer. Don't believe I recognize you. Your buggy's waiting for you, ain't it?

JIMMY VALENTINE turns back to ANNABEL.

JIMMY VALENTINE: Hey, Annabel. Annabel!

VALENTINE runs off to find ANNABEL.

The lights return to the prison pharmacy.

SCENE SEVEN
THE REAL ENDING

PORTER: That man is a blackguard and a crook. Every cent he owns is filthy with the tears and blood of good men. What was his excuse?

JENNINGS: He hid behind the governor. Said it was out of his hands.

PORTER: And I'll wager he fought Dick's corner for all of five minutes. If I could stand against him alone, he'd hit the hay and never wake up.

JENNINGS: What'll we do, Bill?

PORTER: We'll do what we do best. We'll carry on as if nothing has happened.

JENNINGS: We can't do that. Dick won't last in here, you know that.

PORTER: And what would you suggest, colonel?

JENNINGS: We go to Coffin and tell him he's not playing square. Tell him we'll go straight to the Governor if we have to.

PORTER: You do that, colonel, and you'll be signing our death warrants. The man who tries to hurl himself against the tide of humanity is sure to drown, make no mistake.

DICK PRICE enters the pharmacy. He is exceedingly weak and coughs excessively.

DICK PRICE: Hiya fellas. You got that medicine for me, Bill.

PORTER: Got it right here. Now you take care of yourself, you old goat. We can't afford for you to go cracking any more safes.

DICK PRICE: I know Bill, I know. Here I brought you fellas something.

DICK PRICE produces a crumpled piece of paper.

JENNINGS: (*Taking it.*) What is it?

DICK PRICE: It's a list of things I never done. Think of it, Al. I never saw the ocean, never sang, never danced, never went to a theatre. Do you know I never talked to a girl in my life?

Kinda funny, ain't it?

PORTER: Now listen to me, Dick Price. You keep hold of that list and you be ready to start checking it off. The governor might undergo a change of heart any moment.

JENNINGS: And soon as he does, you'll be taking out a different girl every night. There's no age limit at the theatre, least not as far as I remember.

DICK PRICE takes back the paper.

DICK PRICE: Thanks, fellas. You know I'd do anything for you.

DICK PRICE staggers towards his cell.

Why do you suppose I was born, Al?

JENNINGS and PORTER exchange a look. DICK PRICE exits.

JENNINGS: In all the time I knew him, this was the only occasion Dick questioned his lot. Sadly, he didn't wait long for my answer. Dick Price was carted to his grave in a wheelbarrow and buried without a kind soul at his side. He had been chewed up by the system and spat out.

A SINGER appears.

SINGER: Mine eyes have seen the glory
Of the coming of the Lord;
He is trampling out the vintage
Where the grapes of wrath are stored;
He hath loosed the fateful lightning

Of His terrible swift sword;
His truth is marching on.

COMPANY: Glory! Glory! Hallelujah!
Glory! Glory! Hallelujah!
Glory! Glory! Hallelujah!
His truth is marching on.

In the beauty of the lilies
Christ was born across the sea,
With a glory in His bosom
That transfigures you and me;
As He died to make men holy,
Let us die to make men free;
While God is marching on.

JENNINGS: Such was the hopeless story of Jimmy Valentine
as it really unfolded in the Ohio penitentiary. Yet reading
Porter's story, I realized he'd done something special.
He gave Dick Price and inmates everywhere the second
chance we would never receive in life. He gave us a kind
of freedom. A freedom to hope.

COMPANY: Glory! Glory! Hallelujah!
Glory! Glory! Hallelujah!
Glory! Glory! Hallelujah!
His truth is marching on.

He has sounded forth the trumpet
That shall never call retreat;
He is sifting out the hearts of men
Before His judgement seat;
Oh, be swift, my soul, to answer Him;
Be jubilant, my feet;
Our God is marching on.

JIMMY RAIDLER: (*Under the singing.*) Al? Al? There you are!
I've been looking all o-over for you.

JENNINGS: What is it? What's the matter?

JIMMY RAIDLER: Haven't you hard the news? Jack Love got sent down. He's been sent here to Ohio. What you gonna do, Al?

JENNINGS: I'm going to kill him.

End of Act One.

ACT TWO

STRICTLY BUSINESS

A spotlight appears on a VAUDEVILLE MANAGER.

VAUDEVILLE MANAGER: I suppose you know all about the stage and stage people and I suppose that a condensed list of your ideas about the mysterious stageland would boil down to something like this:

Leading ladies have five husbands, paste diamonds, and figures no better than your own, madam. The greatest treat an actor can have is to witness the pitiful performance with which all other actors desecrate the stage.

Latterly there has been much talk of these actor people in a new light. It seems to have been divulged that they are businesslike folk, conducting their private affairs in as orderly and unsensational a manner as any of us good citizens.

The piano plays. Most of this scene is underscored. It is a vaudeville sketch.

I offer you merely this little story of two strollers beginning, as many stories have, in Keetor's old vaudeville theatre.

A vaudeville theatre. BOB HART appears.

Bob Hart had been roaming circuits for four years with a mixed-up act comprising a monologue and three lightning changes with songs.

One afternoon he presented his solvent, serious, well-known vaudevillian face at the box-office window of a rival attraction and got his D H coupon for an orchestra seat.

BOB HART takes his ticket from the VAUDEVILLE MANAGER and sits.

Acts A, B, C and D glowed successively on the announcement spaces…

A stage. A sequence of vaudeville acts.

…and passed into oblivion, each plunging Mr Hart deeper into gloom. But when act H came on…

WINONA CHERRY appears with her act: 'Snooky Ookums'.

H was the happy alphabetical prognosticator of Winona Cherry –

CHERRY: 'In Character Songs And Impersonations.'

VAUDEVILLE MANAGER: There were scarcely more than two bites to Cherry. Bob Hart thought that Cherry seemed exactly to fit the part of Helen Grimes in 'Mice Will Play', the sketch he had written and kept tucked away in the tray of his trunk.

After the act was over Hart found Cherry in her dressing room.

A dressing room.

CHERRY: I know your act, Mr Hart. What did you wish to see me about?

HART: I saw your work tonight. I've written a sketch that I've been saving up. It's for two; and I think you can do the other part. I thought I'd see you about it.

CHERRY: Come in. I've been wishing for something of the sort. I think I'd like to act instead of doing turns.

VAUDEVILLE MANAGER: Bob Hart drew his cherished 'Mice Will Play' from his pocket, and read it to her.

HART acts out the play in ten seconds. He looks at CHERRY exhausted but hopeful.

CHERRY: Read it again, please.

HART looks hopelessly at PIANIST then repeats his act at double speed.

Mr Hart, I believe your sketch is going to win out. That Grimes part fits me like a shrinkable flannel after its first trip to a handless hand laundry. And I've seen you work. I know what you can do with the other part. But business is business. How much do you get a week for the stunt you do now?

HART is embarrassed and hesitant.

HART: Er…well…about two hundred.

CHERRY: I get one hundred for mine. That's about the natural discount for a woman. But I live on it. The stage is all right – I love it. But there's something else I love better. That's a little country home, some day, with Plymouth Rock chickens and six ducks wandering around the yard.

Now, let me tell you, Mr Hart, I am 'strictly business'. If you want me to play the opposite part in your sketch, I'll do it. And I believe we can make it go. But I'm on the stage for what I can cart away from it every payday. I don't know what an all-night restaurant looks like, I never spoke to a man at a stage entrance in my life, I drink only weak tea and I've got money in five savings banks.

HART: Miss Cherry, you're in on your own terms. I've got 'strictly business' pasted in my hat. When I dream of nights I always see a five-room bungalow on the north shore of Long Island and nobody else around.

CHERRY: What I'm going to do with my money is to bank it. You can get four percent on deposits. At the salary I've been earning, I've figured out that in ten years I'd have about fifty dollars a month just from the interest alone. Well, I might invest some in a little business – say, trimming hats or a beauty parlor – and make more.

HART and CHERRY shake hands.

VAUDEVILLE MANAGER: And now for the act itself.

A stage. CHERRY appears as Helen Grimes and does some sharp shooting.

Helen Grimes, who is a Western girl of decidedly Buffalo Billish skill and daring, is tempestuously in love with…

HART appears as Jack Valentine and the two move in for a kiss, when interrupted by:

Jack Valentine, the private secretary and confidential prospective son-in-law of…

Her father, Arapahoe Grimes!

There was another girl in the sketch – a Fifth Avenue society swelless who had sirened Jack Valentine when he was a wealthy club-man on lower Third Avenue.

The STAGEHAND appears as the Swelless, prompting an argument between Valentine and Grimes. The STAGEHAND raises a wooden frame, suddenly becoming a portrait.

This girl appeared on the stage only in the photographic form.

The STAGEHAND raises a wooden frame, suddenly becoming a portrait. HART and CHERRY disappear.

There were only two parts and a half in 'Mice Will Play'. Hart and Cherry were the two, of course; and the half was a minor part always played by a stageshand, who merely came in once in a Tuxedo coat and a panic to announce that the house was surrounded by Indians…

STAGEHAND: The house is surrounded by Indians!

VAUDEVILLE MANAGER: ...and to turn down the gas fire in the grate by the manager's orders.

The STAGEHAND does as he's told.

And now for the thriller. Old 'Arapahoe' Grimes dies of angina pectoris while only his secretary is present.

And that same day he was known to have had six hundred and forty-seven thousand dollars...

CHERRY appears in time to hear this.

CHERRY: Six hundred and forty-seven thousand dollars?

VAUDEVILLE MANAGER: ...in cash...

CHERRY: In cash?

HART: In cash?

VAUDEVILLE MANAGER: ...in his library. The cash disappears at the same time. Jack Valentine was the only person with the ranchman when he made his croak.

CHERRY: Gawd knows I love him; but if he has done this deed...

VAUDEVILLE MANAGER: You sabe, don't you?

The Swelless appears as portrait. CHERRY as Helen Grimes produces her gun.

CHERRY: Robber and thief! And worse yet, stealer of trusting hearts, this should be your fate! But I will be merciful. You shall live – that will be your punishment. I will show you how easily I could have sent you to the death that you deserve. There is her picture on the mantel. I will send through her more beautiful face the bullet that should have pierced your craven heart.

Slow-motion gunshot and reaction. Money falls from the STAGEHAND's mouth.

VAUDEVILLE MANAGER: And she does it. And there's no fake blank cartridges or assistants pulling strings. The bullet goes through the face of the photograph, then strikes the sliding panel and there is the missing six hundred and forty-seven thousand dollars in convincing stacks of currency. It's great.

Of course old 'Arapahoe' had tucked the funds away and, of course, Jack hadn't taken anything. Jack and Helen ended in a half-Nelson –

Grimes and Valentine kiss.

– and there you are.

HART and CHERRY and the STAGEHAND take their bows.

After the show the booking agents signed blank checks and pressed fountain pens upon Hart and Cherry. Five hundred dollars a week was what it panned out.

HART and CHERRY receive a check from the VAUDEVILLE MANAGER.

That night at eleven thirty, Bob Hart bade Cherry good night at her boarding-house door.

A boarding-house door.

CHERRY: (*Strictly business.*) Mr Hart, come inside for just a few minutes.

HART looks about nervously. He is unsure what she is proposing.

We've got our chance now to make good and make money. What we want to do is to cut expenses and save all we can.

HART: Right. It's business with me. You've got your scheme for banking yours; and I dream every night of that bungalow with nobody else around. Anything to enlarge the net receipts will engage my attention.

CHERRY: Mr Hart, I've got a proposition to make to you that will reduce our expenses a lot and help you work out your own future and help me work out mine – and all on business principles.

HART thinks it over and decides to follow her inside.

VAUDEVILLE MANAGER: And now, after so much cracking of a nutshell, here is the kernel of the story: at the end of its second season 'Mice Will Play' came back to New York. At this performance Winona Cherry was nervous. When she fired, instead of penetrating the portrait, the bullet went into the lower left side of Bob Hart's neck. Not expecting to get it there, Hart collapsed neatly, while Cherry fainted in a most artistic manner. The Cool Head, who always graces such occasions, rang the curtain down.

As described, we see CHERRY shoot HART in the neck, then faint. The STAGEHAND confused, does his line.

STAGEHAND. The house is surrounded by Indians!

He lowers the curtain and carries CHERRY off stage.

VAUDEVILLE MANAGER: The doctor examined Hart carefully and laughed heartily.

(*As Doctor.*) No headlines for you, Old Sport. If it had been two inches to the left it would have undermined the carotid artery. As it is, bind it up and go home and you'll be all right. Excuse me; I've got a serious case outside to look after.

(*Himself again.*) After that, Bob Hart looked up and felt better. And then to where he lay came Vincente, the Tramp Juggler.

VINCENTE: (*In a thick Italian accent.*) Bob, I'm glad it's no worse. The little lady is mad about you!

HART: Who?

VINCENTE: Cherry! We didn't know how bad you were hurt; and we kept her away. It's taking the manager and three girls to hold her.

HART: It was an accident, of course. I'm not hurt bad; the sketch'll go on again and she won't lose out half a week's salary.

VINCENTE: Man, are you a human pincushion? Cherry's crying her heart out for you – calling, 'Bob, Bob,' every second! The girl loves you!

HART: Loves me? Cherry loves me? Why, it's impossible!

VINCENTE: I wish you could see her! She's wild about you, I tell you.

HART: It's impossible, I tell you.

VINCENTE: No human being could mistake it. She's wild for love of you. Wake up, man.

HART: For love of me? No, no, no. Sure Cherry came up with a tax break scheme two years ago and we've been married ever since. But that was strictly business.

Now she loves me?

VINCENTE nods enthusiastically.

She loves me! Ha ha. Ooo!

He lets out a cheer, which turns into a wince of pain.

Cherry! (*Wince.*) Cherry! (*Wince.*)

He runs off to find the woman he loves.

As he goes, JENNINGS appears. He has dark marks all over his face and hands.

SCENE ONE
SALLY CASTLETON

JENNINGS: As soon as I got wind that Jack Love was in the pen, I was condemned to the 'bughouse' to keep me out of trouble. Rows and rows of emery wheels spewed out thousands of steel particles, puncturing the convict in the face and the neck. Porter came to my rescue.

Across the grapevine he sent his message. 'Don't lose heart. I'm working. There's a new main finger.'

The new 'main finger' meant a new warden and an entire change of administration. And sure enough, soon after I received Porter's message, I was asked to sing for the prison choir in the chapel. It was the only place in the pen used by men and women inmates alike.

The chapel. The prison CHOIR sings an upbeat song:

CHOIR / SALLY: Shine on Me
  In the Morning
  Shine on Me
  I wonder if the lighthouse
  Will shine on me?
  Well I heard the voice of Jesus say
  'You come on to me and rest
  Lie down thou weary one lie down
  Thy head upon my breast'

JENNINGS: Sally Castleton had a gift in her voice and, once upon a time, sang in the choir of a local cathedral in Hamilton County. Her family managed to exist on what she earned.

The son of a banker in Cincinnati began to attend the services. They were both young and the girl was attractive. It was the old tale. They loved.

After a while, the banker's son came less and less to Hamilton County. Soon, he stopped coming altogether.

Sally ran away to Cincinnati and got a job in a laundry. After the baby was born, she went back to work, but five or six months later it got sick and Sally had to quit work one again. Her funds were very small. She couldn't afford a doctor. She was beside herself with misery.

SALLY sits with JENNINGS in chapel.

SALLY CASTLETON: If you knew how it looked! It had such a dear little white face and the biggest blue eyes. It would turn its head and its poor little mouth would struggle as if it wanted to cry, but was too feeble. I just got frantic. I was afraid to look at it for fear it was dying on me.

One day it took a spasm and I thought it was gone. I didn't care what I did. I would have crawled in the dust to save it.

I went to the bank. I waited outside for him. He came down the steps. I followed, waiting until no one was near. 'Phil,' I said.

He stiffened up as though an electric shock had gone through him.

'What are you dogging me for?'

I caught him by the sleeve.

'Phil, the baby is dying. I haven't a cent. Oh, I wouldn't let you do anything for it if I could only keep it alive myself. I haven't eaten anything but tea and bread for weeks. Phil, will you pay for a doctor for it? It's yours, Phil, your very own. It has your eyes.'

For a minute it seemed to me that a look of exultation went across his face. But maybe I imagined it, for he caught my fingers and knocked them off his arm as though I were a leper.

'It does, does it? Well, if it's dying, let it die. I can't keep it alive. Is it my fault if it wants to die?'

'No, no it's not your fault. But will you help? Will you pay for the doctor – will you help me to take care of it?'

'Say, beat it and be damn quick about it.' I couldn't believe it. I kept on talking and walking at his side. I don't know what I said. Then we passed a policeman. 'Officer, arrest this rag-picker will you?'

JENNINGS: They arrested Sally and took her to the Cincinnati jail. The man had sworn to a warrant charging her with attempted blackmail. The days passed. The case was not called.

The thought of the dying baby was like a hot coal on the girl's mind. She talked to the matron who went out to see the poor little thing.

Meanwhile, Sally was called before the night court but the man did not appear. She was dismissed with a reprimand.

Sally hurried to get out. She ran down the halls but the matron stopped her. 'It's too bad, honey, they brought you in here. You didn't deserve it. I'm awful sorry for you. Honey, I hate to tell you – the poor little baby is dead!'

It was like a blow struck across the face of a little child. It stunned Sally. The baby was dead –

'Listen, honey,' the matron said. 'You can stay here. It won't do you no good to get out. The baby died three days ago. Stay here for a while.'

The door opened and the half-demented creature ran out, one thought uppermost. She would go down to the river.

A light flared out from a shop window, the girl dallied a moment in its warmth. Old jewelery, emblems, silver plate glinted in the show case. In one corner were three revolvers. Sally looked at them fascinated.

She had to wait until noon. She went straight to the bank and stood behind a column waiting for the man. It seemed that every one in the building rushed out at the stroke of twelve – every one but Philip Austin.

SALLY CASTLETON: I began to tremble. I put my hand in my pocket. The pistol was there. Send him out quick, quick. Send him out before I lose my courage.

Proud and magnificent, Philip Austin swung though the door. He walked like a prince.

'Phil – oh, Phil, the baby died! You put me in jail – and it died. It died without anyone near it. It died because you wouldn't take care of it.

He caught me by the wrists.

'God damn you, you little hag – what do I care about your brat! Let it die. Now go – and don't hang around slopping tears at me.'

I jammed the revolver against his stomach.

'You don't care? Oh God! You don't care.' The trigger snapped.

He looked me straight in the eye. He looked startled and frightened, for just a moment and then he went down in a slump as though his backbone had suddenly melted. But he knew I did it. I saw that in his last glance!

Piano music. SALLY returns to her place to sing the spiritual again.

Well shine on me
In the morning
Shine on me
I wonder if the lighthouse
Will shine on me?
Well I heard the voice of Jesus say
'You come on to me and rest
Lie down thou weary one lie down
Thy head upon my breast'

JENNINGS: The girl's trial had taken just one day. The jury found her guilty. She was nineteen. That fact alone saved her from the death penalty.

Surely this was a tale worthy of the genius of Bill Porter.

PORTER is seen in silhouette.

VOICE OF PORTER: The short story is a potent medium of education. It should break down prejudice with understanding. I propose to send the 'down-and-outers' into the drawing rooms of the 'get-it-alls', and I intend to ensure their welcome. All that the world needs is a little more sympathy.

JENNINGS: I told it to him the next afternoon.

The chapel. PORTER and JENNINGS.

(*To PORTER.*) Don't you think Sally's story has real heart in it?

PORTER: It's all right, I suppose.

JENNINGS: All right? Why it's got everything.

PORTER: Colonel, the pulse beats too loud. It's commonplace.

JENNINGS: All life is commonplace. That's just what genius is for – you're supposed to tell it in a way that will do some good.

PORTER: Not all stories have hope in them, Colonel.

JENNINGS: I can't understand you, Bill. You can make something of this poor girl's story, damn it. Stop being so obstinate.

PORTER: I'll tell you why I'm not interested in Sally. She's far better off in here than she ever could be out there. What chance has a girl with Sally's past got in the world?

JENNINGS: Surely, it's not as bad as all that?

PORTER: We have all of us been branded, colonel. When I get out, I will bury the name of Porter in the depths of oblivion. No one shall know that the Ohio penitentiary ever furnished me with board and bread.

JENNINGS holds up a placard. It reads:

'The prison label is worse than the brand of Cain.
When the world once sees it, you are doomed'
– O Henry

JENNINGS will reveal each of the placards, one by one.

The lights go out. In their place, a strobe imitates the effect of a silent movie.

Music: The Temptation Rag

STORY
THE COP AND THE ANTHEM

This story is to be told as if the audience were watching a silent film in the style of Charlie Chaplin or Buster Keaton. The acting style must be bold and gestural, with focus on face and eyes. All thoughts must be turned into gestures. To one side of the stage is a stand showing a series of placards. At certain points of the action they are revealed. 1st placard:

'On His Bench Soapy Moved Uneasily'

A bench. SOAPY, a tramp, moves restlessly. A leaf falls onto SOAPY's lap. It is bitterly cold. 2nd Placard:

'The Wind Blows – If Only There Was Some Escape'

SOAPY struggles with reading the paper in the wind. His hat is blown off. He scrambles around and is seen by a POLICEMAN, who keeps a close eye on him. SOAPY pretends to be a gentleman waiting on a bench.

A rich gentleman appears, looking for a taxi. Another tramp follows him. The tramp gets close to the gentleman to pick his pocket. A COP watches. The other tramp picks the gentleman's pocket as he hails his cab. The COP arrests the other tramp. SOAPY is upset for his friend.

Then SOAPY has an idea! 3rd Placard:

'Prison Wouldn't be so Bad.
I'd Have Food and Shelter'

SOAPY imagines the other tramp being pampered in prison – given rich food, has his nails done etc. SOAPY makes a decision! 4th Placard:

'A Shop Window'

Mannequins in a shop window. SOAPY spies the shop window. SOAPY has an idea! He picks up a rock, throws it in the air a few times for practice then throws it at the window. The mannequins judder. SOAPY eagerly waits for the COP to arrive. Passersby come running along with a COP. SOAPY holds out his hands to the COP in hope of being arrested. But the COP doesn't believe the culprit would hang around and starts looking about for clues. An innocent man appears. He sees the rock and picks it up out of curiosity. Someone spies the man and points him out. The man looks at the COP, looks to the rock in his hand then back to the COP. He shakes his head nervously. The COP raises his baton. The man looks to the audience then starts to run. The COP looks to the audience then chases the man. The passers-by look to the audience then chase after the man. SOAPY looks to the audience, then chases after the COP, hoping to be arrested. They run in a circle around the stage, in Key Stone Cop style chase. Everyone exits the stage except SOAPY, who is out of breath. 5th Placard:

'A Respectable Young Woman'

A respectable young woman appears. SOAPY barely notices her and is about to move on, when the COP appears again. SOAPY clocks the COP. Then clocks the woman again. SOAPY has another idea!

SOAPY sets his hat at a killing slant, does up his tie and moves toward the woman. He keeps checking the COP is watching.

A workman appears carrying a long plank of wood. He is looking for an address to deliver the wood. As SOAPY approaches the woman, the man with the plank of wood blocks the COP's line of sight. The COP does not see SOAPY proposition the woman, nor her indignant response. The woman moves a few yards further on. The workman with the wood disappears and the COP has seen nothing.

SOAPY decides to try again, setting his hat and cuffs. He coughs and hems, smiles and smirks, always with one eye on the COP. The woman is demure as ever, the COP increasingly suspicious. Again the workman appears with his plank of wood, this time going in the other direction. Just as SOAPY makes his move on the WOMAN, the workman blocks the COP's view again. SOAPY kisses the girl. The COP attempts to get underneath the plank of wood, but gets clipped round the head and is knocked unconscious. SOAPY lets the woman go. She walks off in shock. SOAPY turns to the COP hoping to be arrested and is shocked to find the COP unconscious. He turns back to the woman, sees she has gone. Reluctantly, SOAPY helps the COP recover, who is very grateful. 6th Placard:

'Would Never a Policeman Lay Hands on Him?'

SOAPY is miserable. Then, just as the COP is about to leave he bends over to tie his shoelace. SOAPY has another idea! He runs up to the COP, to kick him from behind, slips over and lands on his back. The COP turns, notices and is only too keen to help SOAPY up. SOAPY buttons his thin coat against the wind. 7th Placard:

'On a Quiet Corner, a Church'

SOAPY appears and hears the church music. He is moved. 9th Placard:

'A Sudden and Wonderful Change in his Soul'

SOAPY decides to go straight, to make a man of himself again.

The COP appears. 10th Placard:

> 'What are You Doing Here?'

SOAPY proclaims his innocence but the COP is not interested. 11th Placard:

> 'Vagrancy! It's Prison for You, my Friend.'

SOAPY is led off unwillingly to prison.

The lights return to normal. The church is now the chaplaincy. The CHAPLAIN appears.

SCENE TWO
FORGIVENESS IN THE CHAPEL

CHAPLAIN: Jennings, we're going to pray. Please join us.

JENNINGS: I – I'd rather not, father.

Two CONVICTS appear. One is JACK LOVE.

CONVICT: I tell ya, Jack, there ain't no taste better than…

JACK LOVE appears and stares at a stunned JENNINGS.

CHAPLAIN: Jennings?

JENNINGS: That's all right. You go ahead.

The CHAPLAIN scowls at JENNINGS.

CHAPLAIN: I asked you to join us.

JACK LOVE: Hello, Al. I heard you were here.

CHAPLAIN: (*Looking between them.*) Jack? Do you gentlemen know each other?

JACK LOVE: (*Grinning.*) Come on, Al. God's forgiven me, why can't you?

JENNINGS launches himself at JACK LOVE and the other CONVICT looks on. The CHAPLAIN calls for aid. The prison CHOIR sings 'The Greatest Creator of Them All' as the CHAPLAIN attempts to separate JENNINGS and JACK LOVE.

CHOIR: Well he's the greatest creator of them all, hmmm
　　The greatest creator of them all, hmmm
　　He made the darkness, separated it from the light
　　He's the greatest creator of them all.

The CHOIR become a chorus of CAROL SINGERS. They sing 'Silent Night'.

CAROL SINGERS: Silent Night, Holy Night
　　All is calm, all is bright
　　Round yon virgin Mother and Child,
　　Holy infant so tender and mild
　　Sleep in heavenly peace
　　Sleep in heavenly peace

DELLA walks past the chorus and they jingle a container for change. She apologizes but she has nothing.

STORY
THE GIFT OF THE MAGI

A table. Two chairs. A hat stand. A poorly furnished room.

DELLA has been singing with the carol singers. She takes her leave, continuing to sing as she enters her home, takes off her coat and sits at the table. She takes out a small tin box and, under JIM's speech, counts out her money three times.

JIM: One dollar and eighty-seven cents. That was all. And sixty cents of it was in pennies. Pennies saved one and two at a time. Three times Della counted it. And the next day would be Christmas.

There was clearly nothing left to do but flop down and howl.

DELLA flops down on the table and howls.

Which instigates the moral reflection that life is made up of sobs,

DELLA sobs.

sniffles,

DELLA sniffles.

and smiles,

DELLA smiles.

with sniffles predominating.

DELLA cries and sniffles again.

While the mistress of the home is gradually subsiding from the first stage to the second, let's take a look at the home. A furnished flat at eight dollars per week. It did not exactly beggar description, but it certainly had that word on the lookout for the mendicancy squad.

In the vestibule below was a letter-box

DELLA: into which no letter would go,

JIM: and an electric button

DELLA: from which no mortal finger could coax a ring.

JIM: Also appertaining thereunto was a card bearing the name

DELLA: 'Mr James Dillingham Young.'

JIM: The 'Dillingham' had been flung to the breeze during a former period of prosperity when its possessor was being paid $30 per week. Now, when the income was shrunk to $20, the letters of 'Dillingham' looked blurred, as though they were thinking seriously of contracting to a modest and unassuming 'D'.

Della finished her cry and looked out the window dully at a gray cat walking a gray fence in a gray backyard.

They both do so.

Tomorrow would be Christmas Day, and expenses had been greater than she had calculated. Only one dollar eighty-seven cents to buy a present for Jim. Her Jim. Something fine and rare and sterling.

Suddenly DELLA stands before the looking glass.

Now, there were two possessions of the James Dillingham Youngs in which they both took a mighty pride.

JIM takes out a pocket watch.

One was Jim's gold watch that had been his father's and his grandfather's.

DELLA pulls down her hair to its full length.

The other was Della's hair. Had the Queen of Sheba lived in the flat across the airshaft, Della would have let her hair hang out the window some day to dry just to depreciate Her Majesty's jewels and gifts.

There was only one thing to do.

DELLA does it up again nervously and quickly.

On went her old brown jacket; on went her old brown hat.

DELLA returns to the looking glass for one last look, then:

With a whirl of skirts and with the brilliant sparkle still in her eyes, she fluttered out of the door and down the stairs to the street.

DELLA crosses the street. The CHORUS start to sing carols and ask DELLA for a contribution as she passes. She wants to help but cannot afford to give away one cent.

A sign reads: 'Mme Sofronie. Hair Goods Of All Kinds'. MME SOFRONIE appears.

JIM: Madame, large, too white, chilly, hardly looked the 'Sofronie'.

DELLA: Will you buy my hair?

MME SOFRONIE: I buy hair. Take yer hat off and let's have a sight at the looks of it.

DELLA does so. SOFRONIE examines the hair.

MME SOFRONIE: Twenty dollars.

DELLA: Give it to me quick.

The CHORUS aggressively sings 'Deck the Halls with Boughs of Holly'. We hear the sounds of DELLA yelping, scissors hammering away and see long strands of hair thrown out from behind the screen.

JIM: Oh, and the next two hours tripped by on rosy wings. Forget the hashed metaphor. She was ransacking the stores for Jim's present.

A CHORUS of salesmen attempt to sell their wares to DELLA. One salesman has what she is looking for.

She found it at last. It was a platinum fob chain simple and chaste in design, properly proclaiming its value by substance alone and not by meretricious ornamentation. It was even worthy of The Watch. Twenty-one dollars they took from her for it, and she hurried home with the eighty-seven cents.

DELLA crosses the street, meets the chorus of carol singers, who are singing 'Away in a Manger'. When she gives them her change of eighty-seven cents, they suddenly sing 'We Wish You a Merry Christmas'.

When she reached home her intoxication gave way a little to prudence and reason.

DELLA: If Jim doesn't kill me before he takes a second look at me, he'll say I look like a Coney Island chorus girl. But what could I do – oh! What could I do with a dollar and eighty-seven cents?

JIM is heard on the stairs.

Please God, make him think I am still pretty.

JIM appears wearing a tatty overcoat looking tired and gaunt. His eyes are fixed upon DELLA, and there is an expression in them she cannot read.

DELLA wriggles off the table and goes for him.

Jim, darling, don't look at me that way. I had my hair cut off and sold it because I couldn't have lived through Christmas without giving you a present. I just had to do it. My hair grows awfully fast. Say 'Merry Christmas!' Jim, and let's be happy.

JIM: You've cut off your hair?

DELLA: Cut it off and sold it. Don't you like me just as well, anyhow? I'm me without my hair, ain't I?

JIM looks about the room curiously.

JIM: You say your hair is gone?

DELLA: You needn't look for it. It's sold, I tell you – sold and gone, too. It's Christmas Eve, boy. Be good to me, for it went for you. Maybe the hairs of my head were numbered, but nobody could ever count my love for you. Shall I put the chops on, Jim?

JIM: Out of his trance Jim seemed quickly to wake. He enfolded his Della.

JIM and DELLA move towards each other then stop just before touching.

DELLA: For ten seconds let us regard with discreet scrutiny some inconsequential object in the other direction.

JIM: Eight dollars a week or a million a year – what is the difference?

DELLA: A mathematician or a wit would give you the wrong answer. The magi brought valuable gifts, but that was not among them. This dark assertion will be illuminated later on.

They return to each other.

JIM: Don't make any mistake about me, Dell. I don't think there's anything in the way of a haircut or a shave or a shampoo that could make me like my girl any less. But if you'll unwrap that package you may see why you had me going awhile at first.

JIM draws a package from his overcoat pocket and throws it on the table.

DELLA: White and nimble fingers tore at the string and paper. And then an ecstatic scream of joy…

She does so opening the package.

JIM: …and then, alas! a quick feminine change to hysterical tears and wails,

DELLA does so.

necessitating the immediate employment of all the comforting powers of the lord of the flat.

JIM comforts her.

DELLA: For there lay The Combs – the set of combs, side and back, that Della had worshipped for so long in a Broadway window. Beautiful combs, pure tortoiseshell, with jewelled rims – just the shade to wear in the beautiful vanished hair.

DELLA hugs the combs to her bosom, and looks up with a smile.

My hair grows so fast, Jim!

Then DELLA leaps up like a little singed cat.

Oh, oh!

DELLA holds out JIM's beautiful present.

Isn't it a dandy, Jim? I hunted all over town to find it. You'll have to look at the time a hundred times a day now. Give me your watch. I want to see how it looks on it.

JIM tumbles down on the couch and put his hands under the back of his head and smiles.

JIM: Dell, let's put our Christmas presents away and keep 'em awhile. They're too nice to use just at present. I sold the watch to get the money to buy your combs. And now suppose you put the chops on.

They kiss, DELLA sitting on JIM's knee. The CHORUS sings 'Silent Night'.

DELLA: The magi, as you know, were wise men – wonderfully wise men – who brought gifts to the Babe in the manger.

JIM: They invented the art of giving Christmas presents. Being wise, their gifts were no doubt wise ones.

DELLA: And here we have lamely related to you the uneventful chronicle of two foolish children in a flat who most unwisely sacrificed for each other the greatest treasures of their house.

JIM: But in a last word to the wise of these days, let it be said that of all who give gifts these two were the wisest.

DELLA: Of all who give and receive gifts, such as they are wisest. Everywhere they are wisest.

JIM/DELLA: They are the magi.

JIM and DELLA disappear.

SCENE THREE
IRA MARALATT

WARDEN DARBY's office. WARDEN DARBY, JACK LOVE, JENNINGS and a GUARD.

WARDEN DARBY: I may be new to this penitentiary, gentlemen, but I am no fool. I understand from my predecessor that there is a history between you two. Mr Love, you are being transferred to Leavenworth. (*To the GUARD.*) See that he's packed.

JACK LOVE and the GUARD exit.

You don't have to pray if you don't want to. That's not what you were sent to the pen for. But killing Jack Love will not bring your brother back.

JENNINGS: No, boss.

WARDEN DARBY: It was an oversight letting you two meet like that.

WARDEN DARBY studies JENNINGS.

Porter, get in here.

PORTER appears.

Tell me about Maralatt.

JENNINGS: Ira Maralatt? Not much to say, boss. He's spent the last fourteen years buried in the prison basement, without bed, blankets or light. For a while he was an attraction at the pen. Warden Coffin used to charge citizens twenty-five cents to stare into the cell of the 'prison demon'. He is violent, incoherent and has attacked over a dozen guards.

WARDEN DARBY: I want you both to do something for me.

WARDEN DARBY throws JENNINGS an apple. A haunting voice calls out the wake-up call.

HAUNTING VOICE: Raise up, Boy, Raise up
Raise up, Boy, Raise up
Gabriel's gonna blow his trumpet so loud
Saint's gonna ride to heaven on the clouds
Ain't you goin', ain't you goin', Boy, ain't you goin'

There is a scream, a frenzied scuffle, a booming thud, and a voice shrills out in frantic terror.

MARALATT's cage. PORTER takes out an apple and approaches the cage.

PORTER: (*Softly.*) Hey, Ira. Ira? We got an apple for you, Ira.

JENNINGS: Maralatt made no answer. Porter left the apple on the floor and we stepped back into the shadows. A moment later, a great yellow hand reached out and closed over the apple.

For fourteen years no one had ever seen the Prison Demon eat. His food would be shoved through the grating and he would not touch it. At night, when no one was watching, he would drag it into his cell.

After that day with the apple, Porter and I would return to the basement, bringing with us biscuits, fruit and bread. Maralatt would eat out of our hands and even allowed himself to be examined by Porter. He became an honorary member of the Recluse Club.

WARDEN DARBY's office.

WARDEN DARBY: Well. You've both seen Maralatt. Is he a demon?

JENNINGS: I don't think so. He eats out of my hand boss.

WARDEN DARBY: You go along with this?

PORTER: Boss, the man should be in an insane asylum, not a prison. There's something pressing on his brain. That's my opinion.

WARDEN DARBY: You think it's operable?

PORTER: I'm no doctor but possibly.

JENNINGS: Sure enough, the doctors examined Ira and operated. Three weeks later, the penitentiary had a soft-tongued Hercules in the place of an insensate beast. Memory had returned.

IRA MARALATT's cell.

IRA MARALATT: I was an iron puddler in the steel mills when the strikes hit. I could get no work and my wife was pregnant. I told her I'd be back before the baby was born. She walked me to the gate and I never saw her again.

I got a job in the coalmines. One day a coal car shot along the tracks to the chutes to be filled. At the pillar, it should have switched but instead, it headed straight toward me. Further down the track twenty men were working. The car would have crushed them to a pulp.

I was their only chance of escape. I caught the bolting car with my shoulder and sent it sideways. I smashed my head, I think. I was dragged out and sent to the hospital, where I was laid up for months. When I was well enough, I rushed back to surprise my wife, who'd not heard from me in months. I knew she must have had the child by then. But there were new curtains at the window and a strange face was peering out at me.

I asked the stranger where my wife was. He didn't know. He told me Dora went out alive, but was pretty well done in. He knew nothing of the baby. Told me to go down to the landlord.

I bolted down the path, tore through the streets and reached the landlord's office.

'Where's Dora Maralatt? Where's my wife you put out of the bungalow on the hill?'

The landlord looked at me with contempt. 'Who let this maniac into the office? Throw him out.'

I leaned forward, calmer. Touched the man's hand. 'Excuse me, I'm a bit excited. I've been away. You know me, don't you? I was buying that little cottage on C street. I've been sick. I can't find my wife. Could you tell me where she is? Please? They say you put her out.'

'Oh you're the missing puddler! Well, you've lost the house. Yes, the woman was put out. She made a fuss about it and so we kicked her out.'

'Where is she? Where's she gone?'

'Who cares about your bitch of a wife anyway! Get out of here!'

My balance slipped. I leapt over the counter, I had my hands round his neck, wrenching it back and forth until the skin on the scarlet cheeks was like to burst. 'My what of a wife? Say it again! You thief, say it again.'

It took three officers to break my hands loose from the dead man's throat. I was knocked insensible, thrown into the patrol wagon, and taken off to the station house. I've been here ever since.

JENNINGS: Darby made Maralatt a caretaker in the condemned row and he allowed him to raise canaries in his cell. First he had two, then four, then ten.

Then one day the warden rushed into the office and sent for Maralatt.

WARDEN DARBY's office.

WARDEN DARBY: Sit down, Ira and be calm. I've been up to Cleveland. Ran into the strangest story. Guess you told it straight, all right!

IRA MARALATT: Yes sir?

WARDEN DARBY: You had a wife, you say? Dora, wasn't it? Well, she died – died right after they put her out of the cottage. But the baby lived. She's alive today. She was adopted by wealthy people here in Columbus, friends of the governor and I just happened to talk about you. They thought you were a maniac but I told them the truth.

Ira, go over to the State shop, get a suit and shoes. You're pardoned. I took it up with the Governor. You go out tomorrow.

IRA MARALATT, shocked, puts his hand out to thank the WARDEN.

IRA MARALATT: (*Sobbing.*) Does she know?

WARDEN DARBY: Now, no, they haven't told her. It would be too sudden a strain.

IRA MARALATT: Mr Al, won't she recognize me? I don't want her to know her father was the Prison Demon.

JENNINGS: Don't you worry about it. Take those canaries with you for a present – she'll love them.

IRA MARALATT: I don't know how to thank you, warden!

WARDEN DARBY: You don't have to – God knows you've paid for it.

IRA MARALATT leaves with his canaries.

JENNINGS: A week passed and the warden heard nothing. He contacted the girl's foster mother and within an hour Maralatt's daughter was at the prison.

WARDEN DARBY's office.

MARY: An old man with canaries? Yes I have the birds now. What about them?

WARDEN DARBY: You understand that this man was your father. Your father by birth.

MARY: My father? No he never said – so that's what he meant when he left, calling me his 'Little Dora'. Why didn't someone tell me? Hurry, let us look for him.

The fiddle plays 'The Dying Californian' as MARY and the WARDEN exit.

JENNINGS: Outside it was snowing. Mary and the warden searched in every street and alley and passageway for the old man. He was nowhere to be found. Flinging themselves along in the wind, they finally found him burning up with fever. They dragged him back to the prison, but it was too late.

MARY and the WARDEN are dragging MARALATT back into the prison.

MARY: Don't die, Daddy! Why didn't you tell me? See. I'm your girl, Mary. Oh why didn't you tell me?

MARALATT looks up at her.

IRA MARALATT: I'm so glad you found me, Mary. Please forgive me.

MARALATT dies. A DOCTOR looks him over and confirms it. Someone sings 'The Dying Californian':

MARY: Lay up nearer brother, nearer,
For my limbs are growing cold,
And thy presence seemeth dearer
When thine arms around me fold.
I am dying brother, dying,
Soon you'll miss me in your berth;
For my form will soon be lying,
Beneath the ocean's briny surf

I am going brother, going
But my hope in God is strong
I am willing brother, knowing
That I doeth nothing wrong
Hark I hear the Saviour speaking
'Tis, I know his voice so well
When I'm gone, oh don't be weeping
Brother hear my last farewell

The DOCTOR approaches.

STORY
THE LAST LEAF

DOCTOR: In a little district west of Washington Square the streets have run crazy and broken themselves into small strips called 'places'. These 'places' make strange angles and curves. One street even crosses itself a time or two. An artist once discovered a valuable possibility in this street. Suppose a collector with a bill for paints, paper, and canvas should, in traversing this route, suddenly meet himself coming back, without a cent having been paid on account!

A broken down tenement loft appears. SUE paints at her easel; JOHNSY reclines on the chaise.

So, to quaint old Greenwich Village the art people soon came prowling, hunting for north windows, Dutch attics and low rents. In no time at all it became a 'colony'.

SUE: At the top of a squatty, three-storey brick house Sue

JOHNSY: and Johnsy

SUE: had their studio.

JOHNSY: 'Johnsy' was familiar for Joanna.

SUE: One was from Maine;

JOHNSY: The other from California.

DOCTOR: In November a cold, unseen stranger, whom the doctors called Pneumonia, stalked about the colony, touching one here and there with his icy finger.

SUE: Mr Pneumonia was not what you would call a chivalric old gentleman. A mite of a little woman with blood thinned by California zephyrs was hardly fair game for the red-fisted, short-breathed old duffer. But Johnsy he smote;

JOHNSY: and she lay, scarcely moving, on her painted iron bedstead, looking through the small Dutch windowpanes at the blank side of the next brick house.

The DOCTOR invites SUE into the hallway.

DOCTOR: She has one chance in – let us say, ten. And that chance is for her to want to live. This way people have of lining up on the side of the undertaker makes the entire pharmacopœia look silly. Your little lady has made up her mind that she's not going to get well. Has she anything on her mind?

SUE: She – she wanted to paint the Bay of Naples some day.

DOCTOR: Paint? – bosh! Has she anything on her mind worth thinking about twice – a man, for instance?

SUE: A man? Is a man worth – but no, doctor; there is nothing of the kind.

DOCTOR: Well, it is the weakness, then. I will do all that science, so far as it may filter through my efforts, can accomplish. But whenever my patient begins to count the carriages in her funeral procession I subtract fifty per cent from the curative power of medicines. If you will get her to ask one question about the new winter styles in cloak sleeves I will promise you a one-in-five chance for her, instead of one in ten.

JOHNSY: After the doctor had gone, Sue went into the workroom and cried a Japanese napkin to a pulp.

As SUE paints, she hears low moaning sounds from JOHNSY.

SUE: Johnsy's eyes were open wide. She was looking out the window and

JOHNSY: Fourteen

SUE: counting

JOHNSY: Thirteen

SUE: – counting backward.

JOHNSY: Twelve

SUE: she said, and a little later,

JOHNSY: eleven

SUE: and then

JOHNSY: ten

SUE: and

JOHNSY: nine

SUE: and then

JOHNSY: eight

SUE: and

JOHNSY: seven

SUE: almost together. Sue looked solicitously out the window. What was there to count? There was only a bare, dreary yard and an old, old ivy vine, gnarled and decayed at the roots.

JOHNSY moans.

What is it, dear?

JOHNSY: Six. They're falling faster now. Three days ago there were almost a hundred. It made my head ache to count them. But now it's easy. There goes another one. There are only five left now.

SUE: Five what, dear? Tell your Sudie.

JOHNSY: Leaves. On the ivy vine. When the last one falls I must go too. I've known that for three days. Didn't the doctor tell you?

SUE: Oh, I never heard of such nonsense! What have old ivy leaves to do with your getting well? And you used to love that vine so, you naughty girl. Don't be a goosey. Why, the doctor told me this morning that your chances for getting well real soon were ten to one! Try to take some broth now.

JOHNSY: No, I don't want any broth. There goes another one. That leaves just four. I want to see the last one fall before it gets dark. Then I'll go too.

SUE: Johnsy, dear. Will you promise to keep your eyes closed, and not look out the window until I am done working? I must hand these drawings in by tomorrow. I need the light, or I would draw the shade down.

JOHNSY: Tell me as soon as you have finished because I want to see the last one fall. I'm tired of waiting. I'm tired of thinking. I want to turn loose my hold on everything, and go sailing down, down, just like one of those poor, tired leaves.

SUE: Try to sleep. I must call Behrman up to be my model for the old hermit miner. I'll not be gone a minute. Don't try to move till I come back.

BEHRMAN appears.

BEHRMAN: Old Behrman vas a painter who lived on de ground floor peneath zem. He vas past sixty and vas a failure in art. Forty years he hat vielded de prush. He hat been alvays about to paint a masterpiece, but hat never yet begun it. He drank gin to excess, and still talked of his coming masterbiece. For de rest he vas a fierce little old man, who scoffed terribly at softness in any von, and who regarded himself as especial mastiff-in-vaiting to brotect de two young artists in de studio apove.

SUE goes to greet BEHRMAN and pulls away.

SUE: Sue found Behrman smelling strongly of juniper berries in his dimly lighted den below. She told him of Johnsy's fancy, and how she feared she would, indeed, light and fragile as a leaf herself, float away when her slight hold upon the world grew weaker.

BEHRMAN: Old Behrman, mit his red eyes plainly streaming, shouted his contempt and derision vor such idiotic imaginings. Vass! Is dere people in de world mit der foolishness to die because leafs dey drop off from a confounded vine? I haf not heard of such a thing. No, I vill not bose as a model for your fool hermit-dunderhead. Vy do you allow dot silly pusiness? Ach, dot poor lettle Miss Yohnsy.

SUE: She is very ill and weak and the fever has left her mind morbid and full of strange fancies. Very well, Mr Behrman, if you do not care to pose for me, you needn't. But I think you are a horrid old – old flibbertigibbet.

BEHRMAN: You are just like a woman! Who said I vill not bose? Go on. I come mit you. For half an hour I haf peen trying to say dot I am ready to bose. Gott! dis is not any blace in which one so goot as Miss Yohnsy shall lie sick. Some day I vill baint a masterpiece, and ve shall all go avay. Gott! yes.

Music.

But lo! after de beating rain and fierce gusts of wind dat had endured through de livelong night, der yet stood out against de brick wall one ivy leaf. It vas de last on de vine. Still dark-green near its stem, but mit its serrated edges tinted mit de yellow ov dissolution and decay, it hung pravely from a branch some twenty feet above de ground.

In de morning light dey could see de lone ivy leaf clinging to its stem against de vall.

SUE: When it was light enough, the ivy leaf was still there.

JOHNSY: I've been a bad girl, Sudie. Something has made that last leaf stay there to show me how wicked I was. It is a sin to want to die. You may bring me a little broth now – no; bring me a hand-mirror first; and then pack some pillows about me, so I can sit up and watch you cook.

Sudie, some day I hope to paint the Bay of Naples.

DOCTOR: The doctor came in the afternoon.

Even chances. With good nursing you'll win.

SUE hugs him.

I have to go now. I must see another case I have downstairs. Behrman, his name is – some kind of an artist, I believe. Pneumonia, too. He is an old, weak man, and the attack is acute. There is no hope for him; but he goes to the hospital today to be made more comfortable.

Music. SUE goes into JOHNSY.

SUE: I have something to tell you, white mouse. Mr Behrman died of pneumonia today in the hospital. He was ill only two days. The janitor found him helpless with pain. His shoes and clothing were wet through and icy cold. They couldn't imagine where he had been on such a dreadful night. And then they found a lantern, still lighted, and a ladder that had been dragged from its place and some scattered brushes, and a palette with green and yellow colors mixed on it, and – look out the window, dear, at the last ivy leaf on the wall. Didn't you wonder why it never fluttered or moved when the wind blew? Ah, darling, it's

Behrman's masterpiece – he painted it there the night that
the last leaf fell.

*The COMPANY sings 'My Wild Irish Rose'. SUE and JOHNSY
waltz together.*

COMPANY: (*Singing.*) If you listen I'll sing you a sweet little song
Of a flower that's now drooped and dead,
Yet dearer to me, yes than all of its mates,
Though each holds aloft its proud head.
'Twas given to me by a girl that I know,
Since we've met, faith I've known no repose.
She is dearer by far than the world's brightest star,
And I call her my wild Irish Rose.

My wild Irish Rose, the sweetest flower that grows.
You may search everywhere, but none can compare
With my wild Irish Rose.
My wild Irish Rose, the dearest flower that grows,
And some day for my sake, she may let me take
The bloom from my wild Irish Rose.

SCENE FOUR
SOME GOOD NEWS

*The kitchen. LOUISA is shaving JENNINGS as JIMMY RAIDLER looks
on.*

JIMMY RAIDLER: You nearly f-finished, fellas.

JENNINGS: What's the rush, Jimmy?

JIMMY RAIDLER: No rush, no rush. Only, you think maybe
you could give me the once over, Louisa. When you're
done, I mean.

LOUISA: Sure, Jimmy. Just as soon as you grow some whiskers
on that baby's chin of yours.

PORTER appears.

PORTER: Don't you listen to them, Jimmy.

JIMMY RAIDLER: Hey Bill.

PORTER: Gentlemen, it would appear I have been the recipient of two pieces of good news. You will remember the story I read to you.

JENNINGS: 'It possessed a quantity of jet-black hair and a laugh that rippled across the prairie like the sound of a hidden brook.'

JIMMY RAIDLER: 'The name of it was…'

JIMMY RAIDLER/JENNINGS: (*Together.*) 'Rosita McMullen.'

PORTER: The very same. Well a little magazine going by the name of 'Everybody's' had just acceded to publish it and –

He drops a copy of the magazine in front of them. They cheer, grab at the magazine and almost destroy it in the rush to find the page.

JENNINGS: 'A Chaparral Christmas Gift.'

LOUISA: 'By O. Henry.'

JIMMY RAIDLER: Who's 'O. Henry', Bill?

PORTER: 'O. Henry' is me. I am he.

JIMMY RAIDLER: I don't get it.

LOUISA: It's the name he writes under.

JIMMY RAIDLER: Wh-Why doesn't he write under his own name?

JENNINGS: Sometimes it's easier that way. I'll explain it later, Jimmy. (*To PORTER.*) You mentioned two pieces of news?

PORTER: Ah, yes, gentlemen, the last leaf of the calendar has turned. You are now looking at a free man. That is, as of next Monday.

They stare at him, stunned.

Colonel, I want you to do me a favor. You see it's the going
away suits. They're made of miserable cloth. They melt
in the sun and if it should rain they dissolve. Now when
I came to this institution, I brought a fine tweed suit with
me. I'd like it back as a sort of a dowry. Will you look it up
for me, please? Prison gray is not a fashionable color this
summer.

JENNINGS: Sure, Bill.

PORTER: Well gentlemen, do not be disheartened. You will
make me think you do not wish me to leave this forsaken
place.

JENNINGS: We're delighted for you, Bill.

The others congratulate him as the lights fall on the kitchen.

SCENE FIVE
THE STORY OF THE KID

JENNINGS: There's nothing very aesthetic in the prison soul.

Our celebrations at Porter's success and imminent release
were thwarted by a miserable announcement. The Kid was
to be bumped off.

For days we would know when the electric chair was
due for a sitting. There was that gruesome hubbub about
the prison and they were extra busy in the electrical
department. It takes plenty of juice to kill the condemned.

As the warden's secretary I had to attend and make a
record of the executions. A soft youngster of seventeen
would make an ugly job for me.

I knew the facts in the case. The evidence was strong
against the Kid. He and a boy friend had gone down to the
Scioto River one Sunday afternoon to take a swim.

The Kid came back alone – the other boy was missing. Three weeks later a body was found in the mud far down the river. It was decomposed beyond the possibility of recognition. The face had been eaten away.

The parents of the missing boy looked at the remains, found a birthmark on the decomposed body and established the identity of their son. The Kid was arrested. Witnesses had seen two boys on the Scioto and the Kid was pointed out as one of them.

The boys had been quarrelling. Suddenly the Kid grabbed his companion by the arm, dragged him down to the river shouting: 'I'll drown you for this!' Two men and a woman had heard the threat. The Kid was condemned on their circumstantial evidence.

'Yes, sir, that's true.' The youngster looked at me with his gentle eyes and put his hand on my arm.

'Thet's true, all right – but thet ain't all. Yer see, Mr Al, me and Bob Whitney went down to the river thet Sunday and we got to foolin' and wrestlin' round there and we wasn't mad et all, but maybe we looked like we was. He throwed me down and landed on top er me and I jumped up and yells that to him.

'I sed, "I'll drown you for this." There was people there and they heard it, but we was only foolin'.

'I had to git back to work and I left Bob there and I never seed him again. And after a while thet body was washed up and they sed it was Bob and thet I drowned him and they tuk me into court and I got all twisted up.

'I told them it was all just funnin' and I sed Bob was swimmin' round when I left, but they looked at me like I was lyin' and the judge sed "I sentence you ter die" or somethin' like thet – But death don't skeer me.'

All the time he talked the Kid kept his rough freckled
hand on my arm. I never saw softer, kinder eyes than
those that ignorant undeveloped boy of seventeen turned
so persistently at me. The more he talked the harder it
became to picture him walking to the electric chair. I could
hardly imagine him capable even of anger.

'I ain't gonna show no yeller streak. When I was a kid I
had a li'l sister, Emmy. She was a-skeered of everything.
She was a-skeered to go out, a-skeered to stay home.
She'd hug onto my arm and whisper: 'You ain't skeered
o' nuthin', are yer, Jim?' Then Emmy got sick and the last
thing she did fore she died – she put her hands out to me,
and she said:

'"Jim, you ain't skeered o' nuthin', are you? You ain't
skeered to die?"

'And I ain't. I'm gonna walk right up ter that chair same's it
was a plush sofa 'fore a big fire.'

I had to be in the death cell when the Kid was bumped off.
The Kid loped in between two guards as though he had
lost control of his muscles. I could hear his teeth chattering.
His face was bloodless as flour, and the eyes darted from
the chair to the warden. He caught sight of me. I never felt
so like a beast in all my life.

'Oh Mr Al, good mornin', mornin'.'

His head kept on bobbing at me, so that I could see the
big round spot on the crown where they had shaved the
hair clean. One of the electrodes would be fastened on that
shiny patch.

'Mornin' Mr Al, I ain't skeered – what'd I tell you? I ain't
skeered o' nothin'.'

The Kid's suit had been split up the back seam so that the
voltage could be shot through his body. He was led up to
the chair, his shoulders and his elbows tied to its arms and

the straps adjusted. The electrodes were placed against the bare calves of his legs and at the base of his brain.

When he was finally strapped down, the boy seemed about to collapse as though his bones had become jelly, but he was compelled to sit upright.

Warden Darby stepped up to the Kid and called him by name:

'Confess, Kid,' the Warden's breath chugged out like a laboring engine's. 'Just admit what you did and I'll save you. I'll get you a pardon.'

The Kid sat staring at him and muttering to himself, 'I ain't skeered, I tell yer.'

'Confess, Kid,' Derby yelled at him, 'and I'll let you out.'

The Kid heard at last. He tried to answer. His lips moved, but none of us could hear his words. At last the sound came:

'I ain't guilty. I never killed him.'

The Warden threw on the lever. A blue flame darted about the Kid's face, singeing his hair and making the features stand out as though framed in lightning. The tremendous voltage threw the body into contortions, and as the current went through there came a little squeak from his lips. The lever was thrown off. The Kid was dead.

For a long time the whole prison seemed to be pressed down with an abject and sodden misery. The cons missed the Kid from the patch of sunlight in the yard. They knew he had been bumped off.

With only a few days before his release, Porter was fascinated by the Kid's story. 'Do you think we could ever look into the face of death without a tremor?' he asked me. It occurred to me that Porter was writing a story and wanted to daub the color on true. Sure enough, some time later Porter wrote 'A Fog in Santone', in which a young man dying of tuberculosis gathers as much morphine as is necessary to kill himself and takes the fast train to Santone where, as chance would have it, he ends up in a dance hall in a private compartment with a beautiful young woman.

STORY

A FOG IN SANTONE

A warm light on a table and two chairs. A WOMAN and a MAN are seated there. JENNINGS watches the scene.

WALTER: My weekly letter from home failed to come and I was pretty blue. I knew I wouldn't have long before I died and I was tired of waiting. I went out and bought morphine at every drugstore. I got thirty-six quarter grains, and was going back to my room to take them.

He places the pasteboard box full of grains on the table. MISS ROSA raises the lid, and gives a slight shiver at the innocent looking triturates.

MISS ROSA: Horrid things! But those little, white bits – they could never kill one…

WALTER: Indeed they could. Why, half the amount might.

MISS ROSA: Tell me more about your home and your sisters, Walter.

WALTER: One of them, Alice, is like you, Miss Rosa. Maybe not quite so pretty, but, just as nice, and good, and –

MISS ROSA: There! Walter. Now let's talk about something else.

WALTER: I don't know why it is, but I don't feel as bad as I did. An hour ago I wanted to die, but since I've met you, Miss Rosa, I'd like so much to live.

MISS ROSA: You must, dear boy. I know what was the matter.
It was the miserable foggy weather that has lowered your
spirit and mine too – a little. But look, now.

They look out through the window to a beautiful and unusual
moon.

Talk of death when the world is so beautiful! Do something
to please me, Walter. Go home and say: 'I mean to get
better.'

WALTER: If you ask it. I will.

MISS ROSA: A farewell glass. To your better health, Walter.

They raise their glasses.

WALTER: To our next meeting.

MISS ROSA: Goodnight Walter.

She kisses him.

WALTER: I never kissed a girl before, except my sisters.

MISS ROSA: You didn't this time. I kissed you.

WALTER: When shall I see you again?

MISS ROSA: You promised me to go home and get well.
Perhaps we shall meet again soon. Good night.

MISS ROSA watches him leave, then sits again at the table. She
takes up the pasteboard box and empties its contents into her
glass. She stirs the mix and drinks it down.

JENNINGS turns back to us.

JENNINGS: Once again, Porter was playing God, giving the
Kid a chance to live what might be left of his life. But it
would seem fate was capable of a twist as unexpected
as anything Porter might come up with. You see Porter
wasn't in the prison when the shocking truth came out.
Bob Whitney, the boy whose body was supposed to have

been washed up from the Scioto, turned up in Portsmouth. He wrote to his parents. He knew nothing about the Kid's execution.

The State had made a little mistake. It had bumped off a boy of seventeen for a murder that was never committed.

SCENE SIX
FREEDOM AT LAST

PORTER in a fine new suit. He looks to JENNINGS.

PORTER: Looks like it's time for me to go, colonel.

JENNINGS: Where are you headed?

PORTER: New York, I think. I'm in need of some new stories and I believe Broadway will offer a fresh supply.

JENNINGS: That name you used. 'O. Henry.'

PORTER: Yes?

JENNINGS: Was it...? It's just that...where did you get it?

PORTER: You know colonel, I detest this place. Detest its thick walls, its silence, its cruelty. It is nothing but a concentrate of hatred and defeat. But maybe I'll distil something to take with me. 'O-Hio Penitentiary.' Maybe I'll distil just the name. Take it with me as a kind of memento mori.

Look me up when your appeal comes through.

JENNINGS: If it does. I'll be sure to do that. Take care of yourself, Bill.

PORTER: You too, colonel.

PORTER leaves.

The COMPANY sing 'Oh Freedom'.

COMPANY: (*Singing.*) Oh freedom
Oh freedom

Oh freedom over me!
And before I'd be a slave
I'll be buried in my grave
And go home to my Lord and be free.

No more moaning
No more moaning
No more moaning over me!

And before I'd be a slave
I'll be buried in my grave
And go home to my Lord and be free

JENNINGS: Porter had a sort of corner on freedom
 – a monopoly that was his by the divine right of
understanding. There was in him a sunny toleration, a
freedom of the soul. To have stood at his side and looked
through his eyes has softened with mellow humor the stark
and cruel things – has touched with disturbing beauty the
finer elements of existence.

COMPANY: There'll be singing
There'll be singing
There'll be singing
There'll be singing over me!
And before I'd be a slave
I'll be buried in my grave
And go home to my Lord and be free.

Printed in the USA
CPSIA information can be obtained
at www.ICGtesting.com
LVHW020858171024
794056LV00002B/608